Nosferatu

Director
Friedrich Wilhelm Murnau

Note by Roy Ashbury

Longman   York Press

To Max

York Press
322 Old Brompton Road, London SW5 9JH

Pearson Education Limited
Edinburgh Gate, Harlow, Essex CM20 2JE, United Kingdom
Associated companies, branches and representatives throughout
the world

First published 2001

ISBN 0-582-45254-6

Designed by Vicki Pacey
Phototypeset by Gem Graphics, Trenance, Mawgan Porth, Cornwall
Colour reproduction and film output by Spectrum Colour
Produced by Addison Wesley Longman China Limited, Hong Kong

contents

acknowledgements Thanks to Jenny Rutt of Queen Mary's College Library for finding out-of-print books; Iris Dearden and Michèle Demandre helped with German and French translations; Kevin Brownlow and Lynne Wake of Photoplay Productions gave me valuable advice and kindly found time to look at a draft. Jim Benson (Eureka Video) encouraged me with his enthusiasm for the film.

—///—

author of this note Roy Ashbury is Head of Media Studies at Queen Mary's College, Basingstoke. Before becoming a teacher he was a percussionist with contemporary music and dance groups. Studying Linguistics and Sociology at Essex University, he discovered the 'pleasures of the text' thanks to Peter Wollen's lectures on Eisenstein and the late Andrew Britton's unforgettable Hitchcock seminars. He has written about African Cinema and media representations of 'terrorism'.

background

trailer

this first important film of the vampire genre has more spectral atmosphere, more ingenuity, and more imaginative ghoulish ghastliness than any of its successors.

Pauline Kael, 5001 Nights at the Movies

To watch Murnau's Nosferatu is to see the vampire movie before it had really seen itself. Here is the story of Dracula before it was buried alive in clichés, jokes, TV skits, cartoons and more than 30 other films.

Roger Ebert, www.suntimes.com/ebert/greatmovies

Nosferatu marks the advent of a total cinema in which the plastic, rhythmic and narrative elements are no longer graduated in importance, but in strict interdependence upon each other. With this film the modern cinema was born.

Jean André Fieschi, Cinema: A Critical Dictionary, Roud, 1980

reading nosferatu

Cinema's early years are often ignored by most of today's filmgoers, who mistakenly imagine that it was a monochrome era of slapstick comedy and primitive techniques. It is remarkable, then, when a film made shortly after the First World War can still excite enthusiasm not only among historians but across a much wider audience. How many silent films can equal the role of *Nosferatu – eine Symphonie des Grauens* in modern, intertextual culture? A 'cult movie' for horror devotees, thousands of web sites testify to the interest *Nosferatu* still inspires; there has been a comic adaptation

transcends the constraints of any label

and a musical; 'Goth rockers' and avant-garde jazz saxophonists write new scores for it. While TV comedy performers like Paul Whitehouse of *The Fast Show* spoof its famous vampire, in Wes Craven's *Scream2* Nosferatu makes a sly 'guest appearance'. It was remade in the late 1970s by one of Europe's leading post-war directors, Werner Herzog, and a recent film, *The Shadow of the Vampire*, is constructed entirely around apocryphal stories that have grown up around its production eighty years ago.

It was the first serious attempt to bring Bram Stoker's novel *Dracula* to the screen (at least that survived) and helped to establish the vampire as one of cinema's enduring icons. Its visual rhetoric – its use of **camera angles** and lighting – played an important part in creating the 'language' of the horror film, while Max Schreck's incarnation of the vampire remains an unforgettable performance in the genre's history. But like all great films, *Nosferatu* transcends the constraints of any label. It is a complex film, as much a love story as a tale of terror, and its director, Friedrich Wilhelm Murnau, was one of the most talented and enigmatic personalities in cinema history, whose training in art and drama informed its style and themes. He was 'gay' in a homophobic society and it may be that its narrative, like the mysterious letters that the vampire and his agent exchange in the film, is a coded message of desire and loss.

Few films have provoked such a divergent range of readings as *Nosferatu*. If one wants to understand it, and to grasp how it can be viewed from many different perspectives, one needs to be aware of its history and of the circumstances that were in play at the time it was produced. The film was made at an extremely stressful moment in German history – the country was reeling from the shock of defeat in the First World War and, beset by huge social and economic problems, was struggling to find a new political direction. Paradoxically, it was a 'golden age' for Germany's film-makers, and the company that made *Nosferatu* was one of many that sprang up to take advantage of favourable market conditions as well as the wealth of film-making talent in the country, particularly in Berlin. Successful genres were available for directors to utilise, but they had greater freedom than their Hollywood counterparts to express their individual personalities through their work.

knowledge of the 'black arts'

Of course, the reason that it has survived and can still engage us is its textual power, its visual impact and its compelling narrative. Studying it in context must not be a reductive process of 'explaining away' the text, but one that opens it up to a fuller and more informed response.

key players' biographies

THE COMPANY

Nosferatu was produced by a small company called Prana Film, launched on 31 January 1921 by businessman Enrico Dieckmann and artist-architect Albin Grau. Prana claimed (in *Der Film*, No. 8) a capital base of 20,000 marks and announced an ambitious slate of nine films, principally on supernatural themes, titles including *Dreams of Hell* and *The Devil of the Swamp*. *Nosferatu* was its only production. It was an adaptation of the novel *Dracula* (1897) by Irish writer Bram Stoker, but Prana made no attempt to purchase the copyright. Since Germany's relations with the rest of Europe had not recovered since the War, Prana presumably thought that no one outside of Germany would take any notice. They were sorely mistaken (see Lawsuit in Contexts: Production History).

ALBIN GRAU

Grau was the creative force within Prana, and *Nosferatu* was of considerable personal significance to him. He was deeply interested in the occult and it was his idea to name the company after a Buddhist term for the soul. He was the art designer on the film, responsible for the sets, costumes and make-up, and also for the visually striking **inter-titles**. His knowledge of the 'black arts' is evidenced in the meticulously drawn cabbalistic letters, full of astrological symbols, that he made for the film. His marketing campaign was energetic and featured remarkable expressionistic posters as well as articles in the press.

DIRECTOR

To direct the film, Prana chose F.W. Murnau – now considered to be one of the greatest directors of the silent cinema. *Nosferatu* was his first

modern artists and Berlin bohemia

major success. It marked the beginning of an intensely creative period for him, in which he made some of Germany's most successful and artistically respected films – *The Last Laugh* (1924), *Tartuffe* (1925), *Faust* (1926) – before being invited to Hollywood by William Fox, and given an unusual degree of freedom to make *Sunrise* (1927), a highpoint of silent cinema.

He was born in 1888, as Friedrich Wilhelm Plumpe, to a family of textile manufacturers. In recollections that Lotte Eisner gathered from his family for her invaluable biography of the director, we learn that he was a sensitive child and that 'the dreams that seemed to weave around his being at night surrounded him by day as well' (Eisner, 1973).

Studying art history at Heidelberg, he began acting in student drama productions; he was spotted by Germany's famous theatre director Max Reinhardt (1873–1943) and joined his influential school, eventually becoming an assistant director; there he met many of the people with whom he subsequently worked. Reinhardt was a major influence on German theatre and cinema, transforming the role of director from manager to creative co-ordinator; his productions involved a skilful use of lighting as well as effective **mise–en–scène**. Five of those who worked on *Nosferatu* passed through Reinhardt's tutelage.

Of great importance in Murnau's life as a student was his friendship with a young poet, Hans Ehrenbaum Degele, the son of a highly cultured Jewish family through whom Murnau was to make his first contact with modern artists and Berlin bohemia. Their relationship was probably sexual, although the draconian laws criminalising homosexuality at the time made discretion essential.

It was during his friendship with Ehrenbaum Degele that he changed his name and became Murnau. In an act of personal redefinition, he adopted the name of a small village in southern Germany popular with modern artists. Partly a device to deceive his authoritarian father who opposed his son's artistic ambitions, it was also a way to memorialise a treasured, and probably romantic, vacation he had spent there with his friend. Did he choose the name of a place to give himself a sense of home? We know, from letters that he wrote to his mother when working on *Tabu*, near the

'a pioneer, an explorer'

end of his life, that he saw himself as a rootless wanderer – 'I am at home in no house and in no country' (Eisner, 1973).

During the First World War, Murnau saw combat in the airforce, being shot down several times; it may have been his experiences of flying that gave him a new sense of space and fascination with the moving camera. Sadly, Ehrenbaum Degele was killed in the trenches and his friend's death seems to have had a profound effect on the future film-maker. In *Nosferatu in Love*, a fictionalised account of Murnau's career (but based on extensive research), American novelist Jim Shepard portrays him as being haunted throughout his life by this loss. Many of Murnau's films feature tragic and transgressive love.

He ended the war interned in neutral Switzerland, after a flight in which he lost his way in fog. It was there that he first began to make films for the German Embassy and became committed to a career in the medium; after the war he set up a film company with actor Conrad Veidt, his first films being financed by a German movie star, Ernst Hoffman.

He made nine films before *Nosferatu*: *Der Knabe in Blau* and *Satanas* (1919); *Sehnsucht, Der Bucklige und die Tanzerin, Der Januskopf, Abend ... Nacht ... Morgen* and *Der Gang in die Nacht* (1920); and *Marizza, Schloss Vogelod* (1921).

Murnau was a cultured man, with a poetic sensibility and a painterly eye, whose passion for film-making impressed all those who met him. Wearing a white coat to direct as if he were a scientist, and addressed respectfully as 'Doctor', he could seem austere, but he was fundamentally shy and melancholy. Softly spoken, and sometimes boyishly high spirited, he was far from the hectoring autocrat portrayed by John Malkovitch in *The Shadow of The Vampire* (Merhige, 2000). At his German funeral, actor Emil Jannings, a leading star at the time, described Murnau as 'a pioneer, an explorer. He was always years in advance' (Eisner, 1973).

SCRIPTWRITER

The script was written by Henrik Galeen (1881–1949). Born in Czechoslovakia, Galeen worked as a journalist and actor in Switzerland before moving to Berlin, where he worked for the great theatre director

biographies background

'one of the most tormented imaginations'

Max Reinhardt. He entered the film industry in 1910 and was an assistant to Hans Heinz Ewers, a leading writer of fantastic tales. Galeen co-wrote and directed the first version of *Der Golem* (1913). He also scripted Paul Leni's *Waxworks* (1924) and directed two other important 'terror films' (*schauerfilme*) – *The Student of Prague* (1926) as well as *Alraune* (1928).

Galeen had, according to Carl Vincent (in his *History of Cinema*, 1939), 'one of the most tormented imaginations in the Berlin Studios'. His tastes were not exclusively for the macabre, however; in an essay he wrote in 1929 about the future of fantastic cinema, he revealed an enthusiasm for silent comedy, citing a scene in Chaplin's *The Gold Rush*, when 'the tramp' eats his boots, as an example of how the fantastic imagination could be contemporary (quoted in Bouvier and Leutrat, 1981).

Nosferatu was Galeen's most famous screenplay – a copy survives, and we can see that he wrote in a vivid style closer to prose poetry than to that of a modern film script. In the 1930s he worked in England as a producer on sound films before leaving for the USA in 1933, where he seems to have lost touch with the film industry.

CINEMATOGRAPHER

The principal **cinematographer** was Fritz Arno Wagner (1889–1958), one of Germany's most gifted cameramen (probably assisted by Gunther Krampf).

Wagner had an extremely active career, beginning with Pathé Weekly newsreels for whom he became Deputy Editor in New York in 1913. Returning to Berlin in 1919, he worked with Germany's leading directors. Technically brilliant, he had a realistic style and a preference for smooth camera movements. During the Nazi period, he was under contract to Tobis. After the Second World War he returned to making documentaries and newsreels for *Welt im Bild*. He died from injuries sustained after falling from a camera platform.

American Cinematographer (March 1999) selected *Nosferatu* as among the 50 Best Shot Films in the first half century of cinema (1894–1949) – it was voted nineteenth.

forced to flee by Stalin's purge

PERFORMERS

Max Schreck (1879–1936) could not have imagined that he would achieve a place in cinema history for his performance as the vampire, Count Orlok. He was a competent actor, but never a major star, whose career was divided between the theatre, including a period with Max Reinhardt's famous troupe, and work in a variety of film genres. Tall and thin, even a little cadaverous, he had an angular face, and his strong bone structure provided an ideal basis for Grau's make-up wizardry. Under Murnau's direction, his presence permeates the film even though he makes very few appearances. He worked again with Murnau, playing a comically inept conspirator in *The Finances of The Grand Duke* (1923).

Cast as Knock, the vampire's sinister agent, was **Alexander Granach** (1890–1945). A talented performer, Granach worked for Reinhardt in Berlin after moving from his home in the Ukraine. Jewish and politically left-wing, Granach contributed to Germany's socialist theatre movement, and played a worker in Pabst's film *Kameradschaft*. When Hitler took power, Granach left for the Soviet Union where he acted until forced to flee by Stalin's purge of dissidents in 1937. In the United States he appeared in films (including MGM's comedy *Ninotchka*, starring Greta Garbo, in which he plays Kopalski) but, like many of his fellow German exiles, he was usually typecast in Nazi roles.

Gustav von Wangenheim (born 1895), who plays the estate agent's clerk and Nosferatu's first victim, was an actor from an aristocratic background but who, like Granach, had left-wing sympathies. He too studied with Reinhardt and worked with theatre companies in Vienna, Darmstadt and Berlin. He later supervised a working class choir set up by the Communist Party, one of many attempts at the time to use the arts in political agitation. When Hitler came to power he joined Granach in the Soviet Union; after the war he directed the Deutscher Theatre in East Berlin.

Cast as the tragic heroine Ellen, **Greta Schroeder** was a professional actress who had worked with Murnau on his earlier film *Marizza* as well as appearing in *The Golem* (1920).

The most inexperienced performer was **Ruth Landshoff** who played Ruth. Murnau noticed her walking to school in Grunewald and, struck by her resemblance to a painting he liked (by Romantic artist Kaulbach), asked her parents for permission to cast her in the film during her holidays.

director as auteur

French critics in the 1950s associated with the film magazine *Cahiers du Cinema* considered Murnau archetypal of the kind of director they termed an **auteur** – someone with a distinctive vision of life and a personal visual style, whose films must be interpreted as expressions of artistic identity.

Murnau saw himself as an artist and, in his public statements, discussed the future of film in artistic rather than commercial terms. For example, in *McCall's Magazine*, September 1928, he wrote:

> when a genius in expressing the heart and soul through that tiny strip of celluloid comes to us some day, you shall see that I am right in calling the motion pictures an Art.
>
> *quoted in Koszarski, 1976*

When he worked for UFA, Germany's largest Studio, he was allowed considerable freedom to choose his projects. Given big budgets and the best of the Studio's stars and technical crew, his films were marketed as 'Murnau films' and UFA publicists stressed his genius. When he was invited to Hollywood, William Fox hoped that Murnau's 'European sophistication' would enhance the reputation of his Studio; organising a banquet in New York, Fox presented him to American celebrities as a great artist.

Murnau's Hollywood career turned out, in fact, to illustrate the problems that directors with artistic ambitions have within an industry geared to commercial success. *Sunrise* (1927) received critical acclaim, but performed poorly at the box office, and he soon began to face interference in his work. After two further Studio films (*Four Devils* in 1928 and *Our Daily Bread* in 1929, neither of which were happy experiences), Murnau bought a boat and set off for the Pacific to make a film which he eventually financed himself – his last great film, *Tabu*. Using non-actors he chose from among the islanders he met, *Tabu* was what we would now call an 'independent production' and was probably his most personal film; sadly, Murnau died in a car accident a few days before it was released in 1931, shortly after Paramount had offered him a new contract.

Did he have a distinct directorial style and consistent thematic concerns which link all of his films?

Jo Ann Collier (*From Wagner to Murnau*, 1988), lists what she sees as his stylistic traits:

- long takes
- deep focus cinematography
- use of moving camera
- preference for long shot rather than close-up
- chiaroscuro
- arresting use of shadow and silhouette
- simplicity and suggestiveness of settings
- preference for location shooting
- a tendency to compose within the frame along a diagonal axis
- to minimise titles
- to violate the film frame
- to violate spatial continuity
- to oppose word and image

Many writers on Murnau would recognise these features, particularly his sensitive use of lighting and his complex sense of filmic space. *Nosferatu* certainly contains several of the techniques she includes.

Thematically, Murnau has been described as being preoccupied with 'Oedipal' conflicts – love triangles, and stories that associate desire and death. Even before *Nosferatu* he seemed to be drawn to tragic themes and to stories of transgression in which realism and fantasy often overlapped. Gender identities are often unstable and characters 'doubled'.

film is a highly collaborative process

However, because many of his films have been lost, and even some of those that survive are incomplete, one has to be cautious about making generalisations. His work was diverse, and he did not specialise in one genre. Some of his films have fantastic elements (in *Phantom*, 1922, a man is pursued down a street by shadows), while others are socially realistic (*The Burning Earth*, also in 1922, narrates the conflict between brothers over a piece of land); *The Finances of the Grand Duke* (1923) was a comedy. Many of his protagonists die tragically, sometimes by their own hands, but he could also do 'happy endings'. Some of his films (*Faust*, *The Last Laugh*) were shot entirely in a Studio, while others (*Nosferatu* is an obvious case) made extensive use of real locations. He became famous for the use of camera movement in *The Last Laugh*, but his earlier films only have a few pans and the occasional shot from a moving vehicle. He made films in Germany, the USA and in the South Seas. The budgets he had available were varied. Also, one must recognise that film is a highly collaborative process (this is a major criticism of the auteur approach) – Murnau worked with some of the most creative writers, cinematographers and set designers in Germany and America. It was the dynamic state of German cinema, with its creatively competitive atmosphere, that gave him the opportunity to work continuously and to perfect his skills.

He was also very influenced by other directors. Many of the characteristics for which he is famous are found in the work of directors that he admired. Murnau was most impressed by Scandinavian cinema, particularly by Swedish directors Victor Sjöstrom and Mauritz Stiller. The 'Swedish style' included beautiful outdoor photography, deep focus, atmospheric lighting, and tragic stories.

Some critics see Murnau's style as 'anti-style' – enjoying experiment, he avoided a single approach. Jean-André Fieschi has written that Murnau was engaged in 'a constant refusal to let himself be defined by any particular aesthetic dogma' (in Roud, 1980). Thomas Elsaesser describes Murnau's style as comprising 'under-statement, subtle nuance, humour, allusiveness' (in *Sight and Sound*, 1988/9). Both agree that Murnau's work involved a complex interaction between realism and fantasy, never opting wholly for one of them. For Elsaesser:

an ability to naturalise artifice

Murnau's art, one might say, comprised an ability to naturalise artifice and to heighten reality to the point where the action is suffused with an atmosphere at once lyrical and uncanny, ethereal and mysterious.

narrative

Nosferatu was the first film adaptation of Bram Stoker's novel *Dracula* that has survived (a film entitled *Drakula* was made in Hungary in 1920, but is lost). Inevitably, when discussing its visual style, its representation of the vampire, and its overarching narrative themes and forms, comparisons with the novel and with later films seem appropriate and reveal interesting similarities and differences. Besides minor changes (the names of characters were changed), and the obvious effects of translating a book into a film, there are a number of crucial alterations and changes in emphasis at a structural and thematic level.

synopsis

Nosferatu narrates the journey of a young estate agent's clerk from Western Europe who has been instructed by his sinister employer to help an Eastern European Count buy a property in their town; the young man leaves his wife behind (in *Dracula* the couple are called Jonathan Harker and Mina; in the film, Hutter and Ellen). He travels into an area full of superstitions and popular fears. He disregards warnings and continues to a mountain pass where he is met by a mysterious coachman who takes him to a forbidding castle. There he meets the cadaverous Count (Orlok in the film). To his horror, Hutter discovers that his host is a vampire, an undead creature who lives on blood ('Nosferatu' in Rumanian). The vampire departs for his new home, having seen a picture of Ellen, and the young man escapes the Castle, racing to warn those he loves of the danger that threatens them. The vampire travels by ship, killing the crew during the voyage, and brings plague in his wake. Once he has reached his destination, disease decimates the town. Nosferatu is finally destroyed when Ellen sacrifices herself in order to keep him with her until dawn, when sunlight reduces the vampire to ash.

narrative structure

We can recognise in *Nosferatu* a narrative pattern common not only to many vampire stories, but also to the horror genre as a whole:

Noel Carroll, in his book *The Philosophy of Horror*, identifies a narrative template of four phases which underlies many horror tales; he calls it the 'Complex Discovery Plot':

1) the Onset phase – events disrupt normality.

2) the Discovery phase – a character uncovers what is causing these events.

3) the Confirmation phase – to get help, other characters will need to be persuaded of the danger.

4) the Confrontation phase – the monster is finally dealt with.

However, as Carroll observes, innumerable variations of this basic model are possible. Some stories will dispense with one or more of the phases (so that, for example, the characters who discover the vampire destroy it themselves without having time, or being able, to persuade others of its existence). Phases can be repeated (so that different characters make separate discoveries before finally joining forces). Very important, the events of the story need not be told in a chronological way, but rearranged by the **plot**.

Nosferatu's narrative is broadly similar to that of the novel *Dracula*, and largely conforms to the complex discovery plot (Hutter finds marks on his throat before discovering what Orlok is; the vampire is destroyed at the end), except that its confirmation stage is strangely frustrated – Hutter never successfully conveys his knowledge to Ellen or the townsfolk, nor will he acknowledge her awareness of the vampire; he tries to prevent her from reading the Book of Vampires; Bulwer never links his scientific knowledge to the plague in the town. This is linked to the particular way that the vampire is finally confronted.

SIMILARITIES

Dracula is an epistolary novel – the events are not narrated by a single

multiple narrative voices

narrator, but by several characters who, through letters and diary entries, relate their experiences to the reader.

Nosferatu attempts to replicate some of *Dracula*'s epistolary form – the film opens with the pages of a book, whose narrator tells us that he wishes to recount the story of a Great Plague that took place in the town of Wisborg in 1843; he comments on the action at a number of points throughout the rest of the film. But this is not the only 'voice' that addresses us. We also see shots of what is written in letters exchanged between characters (the vampire and his agent exchange cabbalistic letters; Hutter writes to Ellen). Inter-titles present us with pages of the ship's log recording how the crew sickened and died, while a newspaper headline reports the plague spreading. We read pages of the Book of Vampires, which Hutter disregards but that tells Ellen how the vampire can be destroyed. Both book and film use multiple narrative voices rather than a single voice. Of later versions of *Dracula*, only Coppola's *Bram Stoker's Dracula* (1993) has also attempted (using voice-overs instead of inter-titles) to imitate the novel's formal strategy.

Like *Dracula*, *Nosferatu* sometimes puts the audience in the position of a privileged spectator, able to shift from one perspective to another, and to have a narrative reach (a knowledge of events) much wider than any single character possesses. We see Hutter meet the vampire and suffer his attacks, but are also able to see Ellen's 'telepathic' reaction in her bedroom hundreds of miles away. Nosferatu cross cuts, as the novel does, from place to place and between lines of action: when Nosferatu voyages to Wisborg to find Ellen, a complex montage allows us to see his destruction of the crew in parallel with Hutter's race home, Ellen's anxious vigil, Knock's mounting excitement as his 'Master' approaches, and Dr. Bulwer's lecture on carnivorous plants. This is omniscient narration.

DIFFERENCES

The book and film share a common core, but the differences between them are numerous, some at the level of detail and 'local colour', while others are much more significant.

In *Dracula*, the vampire casts no reflections, while we see Nosferatu's

the physical nature of vampirism

shadow and his mirror image. In the novel, garlic, crosses and holy wafers feature in a vampire-slayer's kit; in *Nosferatu*, there is hardly any Christian imagery (except for the old women who cross themselves at the inn); there's no scene in *Dracula* where the vampire sees Mina's picture in a locket, whereas this is a memorable moment in *Nosferatu* and connects them at an early stage; Dracula dies from a stake in the heart while Nosferatu is destroyed by sunlight.

The book contains scenes of violence vividly described, with the character of Lucy Westenra (Ruth in the film) being violently staked and beheaded while Mina is found drinking blood from Dracula's breast; it has chases, detective work and some vivid action sequences. In *Nosferatu* the physical nature of vampirism is under-stated and largely implied: we see him begin to attack, his shadow, the look of utter horror on the faces of his victims. We see the effects of his presence through shots of the dead captain with two marks on his throat and the endless procession of coffins. The most explicit images are those near the end of the film when he has finally reached Ellen and we see her lying on the bed with the vampire crouched by her side; all we can see in the dim light is his bare head at her neck and his hand, white against her black hair, holding her still. She is motionless. After a shot of a cock crowing we see him in a medium close-up as he relaxes his embrace and his head comes away from her neck to look towards the window where day is breaking.

narration

Nosferatu has a narrator who, in the opening titles, tells us that he is recounting events that really happened in the history of his community. In some of the later inter-titles he alludes to conversations that he had with the surviving protagonists.

He is unseen and was not a participant in the events he narrates. His function seems to be to lend a degree of authenticity to the narrative (just as the opening title of *The Blair Witch Project* claims that what we are about to watch is documentary material) and to provide some information that an audience unfamiliar with vampires might need (that they travel

web of relationships

with coffins containing soil from their homeland). Occasionally he interprets a scene, and even criticises his informants. When Ellen becomes ill, for example, the doctor diagnoses a purely secular disease, but the narrator informs us that the real cause was that her soul had heard the call of the vampire.

Because it is a film, of course, we witness the events narrated on screen and this can lead to tension between what the narrator says and what the audience may feel has happened. We know he is right about the doctor's misdiagnosis, but how does he know what Ellen heard? His words fall short of the complexity of what we have seen. At the end of the film, after Ellen's death, he attempts to close the narrative on a positive note, emphasising that the plague was ended, but having just experienced the dramatic events of Ellen's self-sacrifice, this seems too convenient – a historian's tidy closure on troubling events.

plot

In adapting *Dracula*, *Nosferatu* adjusts, condenses and concentrates the plot:

■ it contains more anticipations and echoes
■ it changes the balance between events
■ it eliminates some of the characters, events and locations
■ it combines some of the characters in the novel into one filmic character
■ of the characters it retains, it focuses only on four – the vampire, his helper, the young estate agent's clerk and his wife – which intensifies the web of relationships between them

In *Dracula* the plot begins with Harker already on his way to Transylvania. He is a little apprehensive and thinks of his fiancée, but has no reason to fear for the future and neither has the reader. *Nosferatu*, on the other hand, starts with a scene that introduces the couple before Hutter knows of the journey. It starts innocently enough, suggesting that they live in a little private 'Eden' of happiness, but soon reveals differences between their personalities (his gift of flowers upsets her) that the rest of the narrative will open up. The next scene introduces Hutter's employer, Knock, who is represented as having some sinister agenda. Using omniscient narration, the audience is allowed to see Knock reading a mysterious letter which Hutter knows nothing about. He calls Hutter into his office and tells the young man that a Count Orlok wishes to buy a house in their little town, and that this represents a great financial opportunity even though it will cost some effort and perhaps a little of Hutter's blood.

He is strangely excited and Hutter seems momentarily alarmed, but only the audience is fully cued to anticipate that there must be an evil motive involved. The **mise-en-scène** is effective here: Knock tells Hutter to look at a wall map and, while he does this in the background, the audience sees Knock in the shot's foreground furtively pore over the occult message. Although our narrative **reach** is less than Knock's (we can't read the letter because it is written in cabbalistic symbols), which creates suspense for us (what is the journey really about?), it is sufficiently greater than Hutter's to know that he is unwittingly walking into a trap. When the young man goes home to tell Ellen, we can now share her premonitions.

The couple's parting is developed in three scenes which deepen our sense that, although they are in love, Ellen is more sensitive than her husband. There is also one shot whose mise-en-scène anticipates the fatal climax – Hutter tells Ellen of his journey and rushes around to begin packing; she stands immobile at the door to their bedroom, clearly distressed; through the door we see the bed on which she will later die, and through the bedroom window we glimpse the outlines of the empty buildings where Nosferatu will take up residence on arrival in Wisborg. After the death of the vampire we will see Hutter distraught on the bed while Dr Bulwer stands helplessly in the doorway.

The film also gives greater emphasis to the vampire's voyage. In *Dracula* we learn of this after the ship has mysteriously beached in Scarborough – through a journalist's account of reading the Log – and we only guess what has happened. In *Nosferatu* the reading of the Log by Harding to the Mayor is used to trigger off panic about the plague; we have already seen the vampire's reign of terror on the ship in one of the film's most impressive sequences, and can see that the town misrecognises the danger. Also, by editing Ellen's vigil at the edge of the sea into the voyage, her relationship to Nosferatu, which began in the Castle when he senses her call to Hutter and when he sees her picture, is carefully intensified.

Nosferatu eliminates the return journey of the vampire who, in *Dracula*, is pursued back to Transylvania and killed before he reaches his castle. In Galeen's adaptation he dies in Ellen's bedroom in Wisborg.

characters

THE VAMPIRE

Much discussion has focused on how Count Orlok in *Nosferatu* differs from Stoker's Dracula as well as from later film incarnations. In the novel we learn that Dracula is tall, with a white moustache, and hands as cold as ice. He has a lofty, domed forehead, massive eyebrows, red lips and sharp white teeth. Pale, with pointed ears, he has squat hands with long, sharp nails. He can be charming, articulate, and hopes to blend into London life once he has mastered the accent and railway timetables. He can turn into mist to enter his victims' bedrooms, but he is also very strong. Cornered, he demonstrates enormous speed and energy. Orlok shares some of Dracula's features (the pallor, sharp nails and pointed ears), but is more spectral, dried-out and leech-like. When he attacks, he demonstrates none of the physical vigour of a Christopher Lee (Hammer Film's famous Dracula), or Lugosi's steely charm in the Universal Studio version. When he first scents Hutter's blood, Nosferatu makes quick, darting movements before 'homing in' on his victim with hunched concentration. Sometimes he scuttles like a cockroach surprised by the light, or like the 'chest burster' in *Alien*, while at other times he rises up and petrifies those who see him with commanding gestures of his enormous clawed hand. At times he is wickedly mischievous – when he invites Hutter to take back Ellen's locket with an amused look, and when he materialises in front of a sailor with his hands crossed over his bony knees. At the end of the film, however, he seems desperately needy, staring yearningly towards Ellen in the hope that she will let him in. Coppola's 1992 version of *Dracula* explicitly develops this idea of inner pain and a hunger for redemption in the chief protagonist – with Mina being the reincarnation of a lost love.

MISSING CHARACTERS

Dracula contains a large number of characters who make no appearance in *Nosferatu* at all; many of these are minor, but some of those eliminated are important in the book. Dracula's three 'wives' are missing. In the novel, there is a highly erotic scene in which Harker is both afraid and aroused by a trio of female vampires who attack him. Nosferatu lives alone, and even loads his coffins by himself – rats are his only companions.

TRANSFORMED CHARACTERS

Even the characters that the film retains from the novel are transformed to varying degrees:

While Jonathan Harker in *Dracula* is a solid Victorian, looking forward to marriage and a respectable career, **Hutter** is already married and sees his journey as an adventure as much as a way to improve his prospects. He bursts with vitality and has a way of rushing through the frame. He loves Ellen but can be insensitive – when he picks some flowers for her, he is surprised she finds this sad. During his journey to the Carpathians, he recklessly dismisses the signs of danger. When attacked, though, he retreats under the covers like a child. Finding the vampire lying in the vault, he never attempts to destroy him. He can be energetic, scaling down the castle walls to escape, but he is ultimately passive – when Ellen points to the warehouse and tells him that she is being haunted every night, he cannot take it in and throws himself onto the bed, as he does after she has died. In *Dracula*, Harker is made ill by his experiences, but he does recover with Mina's help and takes an active part in the pursuit and destruction of the vampire. Hutter is unable to prevent Ellen's death.

In *Dracula*, **Mina** is an intelligent young woman who, although conventional in many ways, is aware of changes in Victorian society that might open up greater opportunities for women. She is unafraid of technology (she uses a typewriter), and has an enquiring mind. She plays a

a lonely act of supreme self-sacrifice

very active role in the novel, particularly in editing information together that helps defeat the vampire. While Ellen embroiders *I love you*, Mina uses a typewriter to 'stitch' together the diaries of her lover and Dr Seward to help Van Helsing. She becomes a victim, falling under Dracula's influence when he forces her to drink blood from his breast, but is finally saved and plays a part in Dracula's downfall when Van Helsing exploits her telepathic link to the Count.

Ellen's character is elusive. At the start of the film she seems child-like, playing with a kitten at her window box, but later we realise that this is part of her affinity to nature. She is extremely sensitive, reacting with unusual sadness when Hutter brings her cut flowers; unlike her husband, who moves energetically, she is often still – sitting at the window with her sewing, sitting at the edge of the sea; only once does she move rapidly in the frame, when Hutter leaves her with his friends and she runs after him for a final embrace. But although she may be physically inactive, the film suggests that she is alert at some deeper, metaphysical level. When Hutter is in danger, she senses it and begins to sleepwalk; when he is attacked, she feels it and cries out. At the end of the film, only Ellen can defeat the vampire and the plague he has brought – not by assisting the men of the town (who are wasting energy chasing Knock) but by a lonely act of supreme self-sacrifice.

Of particular significance is how two of the most important people in Stoker's tale are drastically marginalized in the film – the characters of Lucy Westenra and Doctor Van Helsing: The film differs markedly from *Dracula* in the role played by Ellen's friend (Lucy in the book, Ruth in the film). In the novel she is an important character whose personality and fate have provoked much debate. Lucy is a pretty and flirtatious member of the aristocracy. Dracula transforms her into an eroticised vampire preying on small children (the 'Bloofer Lady'). She is destroyed in one of the most graphic scenes in the novel, staked through the heart and decapitated by the men who once loved her. Many critics of the book have interpreted this as symptomatic of Stoker's Victorian fears of female sexuality. In *Nosferatu*, **Ruth** is a minor character – she is devoted to Ellen, but they have very few scenes together, and her death is handled in an extremely understated way (a curtain stirs in the wind, a candle is blown out). She is simply an innocent victim.

Bulwer, the Paracelsian doctor in *Nosferatu*, is no match for *Dracula*'s Dr Van Helsing. Van Helsing is a powerful and patriarchal character in the novel, whose knowledge and energy are central to defeating the dark patriarch from Transylvania. Bulwer, by contrast, is knowledgeable but ineffectual. He lectures his students on carnivorous plants and the violence inherent in nature, but he fails to use his expertise against *Nosferatu*. At the end of the film narrative he stands helpless, uncomfortable in the frame.

POINT OF VIEW

Whose story is it? It is told by a town archivist, but he is only the scribe. At first it seems to be Hutter's story, since we experience his journey into danger and discover the Count's real identity when he does (although the cabbalistic letter and Knock's behaviour make us uneasy). It then becomes Ellen and Nosferatu's story as the film focuses on her vigil and his relentless progress towards her. This builds towards the climactic encounter in which both of them will die, a process in which Hutter becomes an onlooker.

ambiguity

In *Dracula* there is no suggestion that Mina awaits the vampire and/or that she desires him. Only after she has been forced to drink his blood does she feel sympathy for him. In *Nosferatu* several critics perceive ambiguity in Ellen's relationship to the vampire. When she tells Ruth that she must go to him, does she mean Hutter or Nosferatu? Scenes of her looking out to sea are followed not by shots of Hutter travelling by land but of the ship on which Nosferatu is the new captain. When she embroiders *Ich Liebe Dich*, is it Hutter that she means or the vampire?

not a conventional 'happy ending'

destruction of the vampire

A central difference between the book and the film is in their narrative resolutions:

In *Dracula*, a collective effort by characters who are represented as forces of good destroys the vampire. The knowledge and experience they gain enables them to end his reign of terror. It's a close-run thing, which gives the story its breathless excitement, but the characters learn from what happens to them, and Van Helsing's knowledge is effective. Normality is restored through a combination of wisdom and violence. The novel has a strong narrative closure.

In *Nosferatu*, the vampire dies – but not through detective work and the application of knowledge acquired through experience; it is not thanks to the leadership of authoritative men and no collective effort is involved. Rational authority is ineffective in *Nosferatu*. Evil is destroyed only when a woman sacrifices herself. She does this alone, having deliberately sent her husband out of danger, and is aware of the fatal consequences.

The final scene is a closure of the narrative (the vampire is dead and the plague ended), but it is certainly not a conventional 'happy ending'. Ellen is dead and her husband is distraught at her side. The community has been saved, but we see no evidence of celebration. This differs both from the conclusion of the novel, in which we read that Mina and Jonathan have a son, and from the endings of many later vampire films.

style & form

No one who sees the restored film on a big screen, with its colour tinting in place and James Bernard's dramatic score, can fail to be surprised at its power. Beautifully shot, combining effective Studio sets and impressive real locations, it exploits light and shadow to great psychological effect. The editing is assured, and the 'race against death' sequence demonstrates how **montage** can be both rhythmical and thematically complex. Schreck's and Granach's performances are compelling, and most of the effects still have an uncanny quality.

Several of its images have become quotable icons of the horror genre. But this should not obscure the film as a whole. Indeed, its celebrated elements work as effectively as they do only because they are woven into a complex visual texture, and they achieve their full impact and meaning only when seen in the context of the narrative as a whole.

visual style

The visual style of a film comprises a number of inter-related features – sets and locations, costumes, performances, lighting (the **mise-en-scène**) as well as the use of the camera, editing and other results of post-production. In the case of a silent film, there are also **inter-titles** which can make a visual contribution as well as convey information.

uncanny atmosphere

sets & locations

Unlike many German films of the time, and unlike the first Hollywood *Dracula* (1931), much of *Nosferatu* was shot outside a Studio. Hutter rides out of a real sun-filled square, travels into formidably real mountains and meets the vampire in a genuine castle with no cardboard bats in sight. While Hollywood horror films of the 1930s look artificial, with fake-European sets and toy boats bobbing in Studio tanks, *Nosferatu* was shot in Baltic ports and the vampire's sea voyage filmed using a real schooner. Nature participates in the drama and the supernatural is grounded in reality. The uncanny atmosphere of the film derives from the way that the naturalistic is subverted by the surreal.

Even the interior sets are naturalistic rather than highly stylised. For a film commonly labelled 'expressionistic', *Nosferatu* has no scenes that suggest a wholly imaginary world or subjective delusion. On the contrary, the sets are economical and restrained. Murnau believed in subordinating sets to actors, in using sets not as passive background nor as intrusive ornamentation, but as a means to articulate character and narrative.

Nosferatu has no expensive sets to compare with those in Murnau's later Studio films like *Faust*, but they are effective and subtly expressive: the hall of Nosferatu's castle is simple, but the chequered floor, its lines cutting across the scene diagonally, gives the scene of Hutter's first meal great depth as well as suggesting a chess game in which Nosferatu is the 'grand master'. Knock's cell, with its bare, scratched walls and single barred window is a stark setting for his madness.

A striking feature of the settings, that links both the real locations and the constructed sets, is the repeated presence of arches: when Hutter arrives at Nosferatu's castle, he walks through arches to meet the vampire who has himself just appeared from out of a tunnel; when they meet we see the two of them framed in concentric arches. The curves of the arches add visual intensity to scenes, by framing them and guiding our eyes towards the characters, but also give material form to the threat closing around the innocent traveller.

doors of discovery

Bridges and doorways are used to emphasise that a character is passing from one psychological state to another. When Hutter is about to meet the vampire and leave behind the world of normality, he crosses a bridge. Doors and other openings are a recurrent feature of the film and emphasise moments of revelation as well as transgressions – inside the castle, Hutter will pass through many doors of discovery, as well as suffer invasions of his space; at the end of the film, Ellen throws open her bedroom window as a sign that she will allow him to enter, and when he arrives he pauses before her closed door, underlining the act of violation he is about to commit.

Like bridges and doors, stairs involve transitions in space and visually highlight important narrative moments; they dramatise psychological 'ascents' and 'descents': Hutter descends the stairs of his friends' home to leave for Transylvania; he descends flights of stairs to find the vampire in his coffin; the mate goes down stairs to confront the vampire in the hold of the ship; when Nosferatu arrives in the port of Wisborg, he climbs up out of the hatchway; and his shadow floats up a flight of stairs before the fatal assault upon Ellen.

costumes, make-up & performance

Costumes and make-up, facial expressions and body language help us to 'read' characters and their relationships.

Nosferatu and Knock are the two 'stylised' characters, with their ill-fitting clothes and exaggerated features. Both are bald, with eyes heavily emphasised by black outlines and tufty eyebrows. Grau's make-up for Max Schreck has always attracted praise; using putty, he built on the actor's features to create an unforgettable rat-like visage. In the scene where Nosferatu terrorises the sailor in the hold of the ship, his hands look enormous – they must have been specially made props. His nails get longer in every scene. His tight jacket exaggerates his skeletal form. Knock has clothes that look too small for him and out of which he seems likely to burst at any time. Their movements are equally stylised – they are

movements seem to obey secret forces

sometimes seen at rest (Knock reads a letter, Nosferatu stands waiting for his guest), but can suddenly jolt into life like puppets whose strings have been violently tugged (Knock explodes into laughter when he tells Hutter about his journey, and makes an unexpected attack on the warder; Nosferatu is as fast as a snake when he smells blood, and rises up from his coffin like a jack-in-the-box). Their movements seem to obey secret forces.

The other characters wear believable period costumes, but which also reveal their personality and status. Hutter is flamboyant, a 'dandy' with a ruffled collar and ornate waistcoat. He is coded as 'effeminate'. Ellen is initially dressed in black, but is in a white night dress when she sleepwalks and encounters the vampire, contrasting her daytime status as a respectable housewife with her nocturnal 'adventures'. Unlike Ruth, her eyes are darkly outlined – which makes her ghost-like in some scenes and links her to Nosferatu.

camerawork

In his final German film *The Last Laugh*, Murnau was celebrated for encouraging his cameramen to devise ways of moving the camera and for the use of long takes. Wagner's work for Fritz Lang features beautiful tracking shots. In *Nosferatu*, however, except for a couple of surveying pans, and shots of the schooner from another boat (and possibly a sea plane), the camera does not move. Rather, at this point in their careers, he and Wagner relied on the use of different camera set-ups, varying shot size and angles, lighting and the careful staging of the action in space. The scenes are constructed from a number of relatively short shots from different set-ups, edited together so that actions flow smoothly and character relationships are made clear.

Barry Salt argues that shot durations in German films of the 1920s were longer on average than in American films, which would account for perceptions that they were 'slow', but *Nosferatu* moves fairly rapidly – the whole film has over 500 shots (I count 545 shots in the most fully restored version).

a coherent sense of space and progression

Consider the scene when Hutter first dines in Nosferatu's castle: It opens with a wide establishing shot of the Hall, which shows them sitting at a table in the middle ground. Behind them, through an arch, is another space with a large empty fireplace. The foreground is empty, but chequered tiles cut across the floor diagonally, energising the space. It is a strong composition in depth. We then cut to a medium shot of Hutter looking up from his food, his gaze to the right of the frame. This is answered by a reverse shot, from his point of view, of Nosferatu reading. We cut back to Hutter beginning to cut a loaf. There is now a close-up of Nosferatu with the letter masking most of his face, except for his extraordinary eyes outlined in black and topped by demonic eyebrows. A medium close-up follows – of Hutter staring in astonishment. A close-up now reveals a bizarre clock with a skeleton figure sounding midnight. Hutter, in the same medium close-up as before, now looks to his left. Another close-up of the clock confirms that it is this that has startled him. A slightly wider shot shows him continuing to cut the loaf, an action he had started in the fourth shot of the sequence. A close-up now shows the knife draw blood from his thumb. In a shot of the table from the same angle as the establishing shot, but closer to them, Nosferatu reacts to the blood by reaching towards Hutter. As he stands up, a shot from behind Hutter's chair picks up the action so that we can see Nosferatu's expression of complete fixation on the blood.

The scene, up to this point, uses 13 shots, each one leading with dramatic logic to the next. Our attention is carefully guided through the scene and a coherent sense of space and progression of events is constructed.

camera angles

Like Hitchcock, who admired the German director and saw him at work in the UFA Studio, Murnau uses angles expressively. One of the most memorable scenes in the film is when Nosferatu attacks the captain of the *Empusa*. He has left his coffin in the hold and come up on deck where the captain is lashing himself to the ship's wheel. Instead of using a camera set up on deck, two extreme low angle shots taken from deep inside the ship's hold show him, clawed hands outstretched, against the sky and the ship's

'... the camera represents the eye of a person'

rigging as he skirts the open hatchway. The vampire's power is vividly represented and the angle highlights the ship's rigging, echoing the spider web which we have seen in Knock's cell shortly before.

Low angle shots are also used of the castle and the warehouse in Wisborg where Nosferatu takes residence. They look more intimidating as a result.

Equally effective use is made of **high angle shots** – when Hutter looks out of his bedroom in the castle, an extreme high angle shot of the gorge below underlines his entrapment; when, later in the film, Ellen looks from her window into the street below, the angle exaggerates the narrowness of the streets in which the inhabitants are now victims of plague.

Murnau was conscious of his technique and responded to critics in his McCall's magazine article *Films of the Future* (September 1928):

> They say that I have a passion for 'camera angles'. But I do not take trick scenes from unusual positions just to get startling effects. To me the camera represents the eye of a person, through whose mind one is watching the events on the screen ... they help to photograph thought.

composition

Scenes in a film can vary in the degree of depth they have. Sometimes space is flat (for example, a character is standing against a wall), while at other times it may be deep (for example, a long room). Within the space are things at different distances, especially if the space is a deep one, and different lenses and lens settings allow a film-maker to select what is in focus and how much of what is in the scene is sharp. **Shallow focus** compositions select things at a particular distance for us to see clearly, while **deep focus** shots allow our eyes to roam through a scene and to see what is going on both near and far. While telephoto lenses are highly selective in what they can keep in focus, wide angle lenses allow deep focus. In *Nosferatu*, there are no shallow focus shots, where an object in the foreground is sharp and the background is wholly out of focus, but there is a kind of oscillation between shallow scenes and scenes with depth. Space seems to breathe, open and close. The very first shot of the film is a **high angle shot** of the town with tiny figures walking about, while the next shot shows Hutter, in a medium close-up, getting dressed in front of a mirror. He walks to work, in a **long shot** of a sunny street, but he is soon in the claustrophobic office of his sinister employer. Later in the film he travels through the awesome wide-open spaces of the Carpathians before finding himself trapped in the Castle, cowering in bed as the vampire advances.

Murnau makes powerful use of scenes in depth to dramatise the relentless advance of evil: when the vampire first appears he approaches from the dark of a tunnel and comes into the middle ground. When Hutter sees him at midnight through the door of his bedroom, he is standing in the depth of the shot and, when he begins his attack, he approaches the foreground straight at us.

Many of the spaces in the film have recesses at the back or open windows to the side. Sometimes they contain obstacles or frames to make them more multi-layered – when we see Ellen sleepwalk on the balcony, it is from the far end of her bedroom and through French windows. Space in the film is a labyrinth.

lighting

Of all the resources used in the film, light and shadow play a key role. The narrative begins in sunshine. When Hutter picks flowers for Ellen, and when he walks to work, the light sparkles. During his journey to the Carpathians, the film looks more 'impressionist' than 'expressionist' as trees rustle in a soft breeze and leaves catch the light. All the more powerful, then, when the sinister coach takes him through a forest of reversed tonal values and into a sinister 'shadow world'.

Murnau's semiotics of light and shadow is skilfully demonstrated when Nosferatu attacks Hutter in his bedroom: the young man is looking lovingly at the locket containing Ellen's picture (which, in the previous scene, had fallen from his bag and was greedily eyed by the vampire). He hears

a highly atmospheric shot

midnight strike on the skeleton clock and warily opens the door to look out. In a powerful shot of the hall, mostly in darkness, we see the vampire standing immobile against the distant fireplace in a pool of light. He is bareheaded for the first time and his outstretched hands are white against his dark clothes. Hutter slams the door and runs to the window, only to see a vertiginous chasm below (tinted blue). Candlelight flickers in the room. He retreats to the bed. The door of the room opens – to reveal the tiled floor receding into darkness. Hutter presses himself against the headboard of the bed, his head circled in light. The open door is flooded with an unusually intense beam of light from screen left through which the vampire advances from the dark of the hall until he occupies the whole doorway. Unlike the use of light in more realistic moments of the film, this light has no motivation; it is unreal and the vampire seems projected by it into the room. We now cut to Ellen in bed, waking suddenly and sitting upright. She gets up and crosses the darkened room wearing a white nightdress. The room has a balcony which is lit so that we can see her sleepwalking on the balustrade in a highly atmospheric shot (suggesting moonlight). When we cut back to Hutter, cowering on his bed, we see on the headboard above him the shadow of Nosferatu's head, with its sharply pointed ears, and of his predatory hands.

Towards the end of the film, when Ellen finally resolves to sacrifice herself to the vampire in order to destroy him, light and shadow are used in a way that echoes but also develops their role in the attack on Hutter: Nosferatu is watching her longingly from his window, his face and hands standing out against the darkness behind him. Ellen agonises over what to do, but finally throws open her window to let in the darkness. When he arrives, it is his shadow that flits up the stairs and stands at her bedroom door. He reaches towards it and his arm, with its clawed hand, seems to take on a life of its own. He has become a disembodied shadow. Ellen looks towards the door and we assume he has entered by her shocked expression and her retreat to her bed. The shadow of his hand moves up her body until it covers her heart; as it clenches, she convulses in pain or ecstasy (see Interpretations: Psychoanalytical readings).

Barry Salt dates the use of shadow effects to around 1915 (in American films like *The Cheat* by Cecil B. De Mille). In German cinema, several films employed shadows thrown upon walls. In *The Cabinet of Dr Caligari* we see the shadow of the somnabulist Cesare use a dagger to murder a young man. In Fritz Lang's *M* a little girl is bouncing a ball against a pillar when the serial killer's shadow suddenly falls across it.

Throughout history, in art but also in philosophy and religious symbolism, the shadow has been invested with a range of complex meanings. While it can represent our tendency to confuse reflections with reality, it is often used to signify evil and the 'night side' of the human personality.

If darkness connotes evil, then light can signify hope and redemption through love. The film begins in sunlight but, when night falls on the Carpathians, evil reigns. At the end of *Nosferatu*, the vampire realises too late that dawn is breaking. He separates himself from Ellen's body, and attempts to leave her room; as he passes the open window, the sky lightens and his body de-materialises into a puff of smoke. The final shot of the film reveals his castle now in ruins against early morning light.

editing & montage

For much of the film, shots are edited for continuity in a 'classical' way. Scenes are constructed out of shots which link logically and which create a coherent sense of space and time. If a character starts an action in one shot, the next one will complete it (match on action); if a character looks screen right, the following shot will reveal what is being looked at; if a coach exits screen left, the next shot will also show it moving left. Murnau never confuses the audience about screen direction (180 degree rule).

Straight cuts are used within scenes, but the film makes extensive use of a technique that was popular in the silent era but no longer widely used – iris in/iris out effects. To close a scene, and to show that a transition is being made to another place or time, the screen 'closes down' to black before 'opening up' again.

Only one dissolve is used – when Hutter sees the vampire across the Hall at midnight, a long shot is followed by a dissolve to a closer shot that acts like a jump cut and enhances his presence in the frame.

However, the film also contains more complex editing which subverts the conventions of continuity editing. This first occurs when Nosferatu's attack on Hutter is intercut with Ellen sleepwalking. For the first time, two separate spaces and actions are linked. We are encouraged to infer from this that Ellen senses the danger that threatens her husband. The two scenes develop in parallel, which was a technique used by many directors to create excitement (the last minute rescue), but which here creates a different kind of connection. Ellen reaches towards the left of the screen and cries out to her distant husband. At this point Nosferatu interrupts his attack and turns to look screen right. The editing puts the vampire and Ellen into an eyeline match, 'facing one another', although they do not occupy the same physical space. The vampire has 'heard' her cry and will now be able to 'lock on' to the signal he has intercepted. A technique normally used to create a relationship between two characters in a common space has been hijacked for a different purpose. The vampire and Ellen are now in psychic contact and space has been 'interiorised'.

More complex still is the remarkable sequence of Nosferatu's voyage. Like a piece of polyphonic music, with several melodies woven together (is this why the film is called a Symphony?), the inexorable progress of the ship, over which he seizes control, is edited into a montage with four other lines of action:

1. Ellen sits staring out to sea, yearning for news of her husband. At night she sleepwalks.

2. Knock, in the cell of a mental asylum, becomes more deranged as his master approaches. He shows his warders a spider catching a fly in its web.

3. Dr Bulwer demonstrates carnivorous plants and animals to his students.

4. Hutter, having escaped the castle, recovers in hospital and then, on horseback, makes a desperate effort to get home before the vampire reaches his wife.

a highly intertextual film

Each line of action 'builds up', but edited together they create an impressive tapestry of meanings.

It is a 'race against time' sequence, but it is also an example of what Eisenstein called 'intellectual montage' – the editing creates a web of associations. Bulwer's lecture on vampires in the plant and animal kingdoms encourages us to 'read' Nosferatu as a manifestation of nature itself – the Venus flytrap preys on living things and its spiky 'fingers' close on its victims just as Nosferatu's do; he can make himself transparent like the polyp; and he travels with boxes full of earth with rats for companions.

A PAINTERLY FILM

Beautifully photographed, *Nosferatu* is suffused with Murnau's artistic sensibility. Lotte Eisner placed Murnau in the tradition of German Romanticism, and a number of writers have pursued connections between his films and works of art.

Angela Dalle Vache and French critics Bouvier and Leutrat consider *Nosferatu* to be a highly **intertextual** film, tracing a number of its shots to specific pictures:

The opening shot of Wisborg evokes a painting entitled *The Blue Church* by Ludwig Kirchner. The shot of Harding at his desk (as Ellen sleepwalks) looks remarkably similar to a picture by Kersting called *The Elegant Reader*. When Ellen looks out to sea, one is reminded of paintings by Caspar David Friedrich in which figures, their backs to us, stare yearningly into the far distance. When the vampire crosses the river to the warehouse, gliding on a shallow-bottomed boat, the scene evokes a painting by Arnold Bocklin called *Isle of the Dead*. When the vampire feeds on Ellen in her bed, paintings by Fuseli come to mind.

documentary realism

In contrast to the painterly scenes, the film also has documentary moments – during Dr Bulwer's lecture we see shots of a Venus flytrap which could belong to the 'actuality films' that Wagner shot for Pathé, there's a shot of a spider at work in its web, and the scenes of the sea and mountains could belong in a travel film.

effects

A distinctive feature of the film's style is its use of special effects to convey the supernatural. When the vampire's coach collects Hutter, and when he loads his coffins on a cart to leave for Wisborg, accelerated motion is used (achieved by under-cranking the camera). As the coach takes Hutter up to the castle for the first time, it enters a wood and the image is transformed into negative, reversing its tonal values to signify abnormality (the coach must have been painted white for it to register as black in negative). On board the ship, a sailor sees Nosferatu materialise in front of him, through the use of superimposition. In one of the most unforgettable scenes in the film, when the ship's mate smashes open coffins to investigate the source of plague and terror, Nosferatu rises rigidly up into a standing position, which was presumably achieved by filming Schreck falling backwards and then reversing the shot. Critic Roger Ebert comments that this scene was as shocking in its time as the rotating head sequence in The Exorcist years later. Stop–motion is used when Nosferatu appears out of the hold of the ship of death – the tarpaulin magically rolls back. In the final scene, of Nosferatu's destruction, he is dematerialised and stop-motion allows his body to become a puff of smoke.

These effects were probably done in the camera (by changing its speed or by rewinding the film and re-shooting). We know from the script that some of the effects were indicated by Galeen (e.g. that the coach should move with unearthly speed) while others (the use of negative, for example) were added by Murnau.

Earlier German films of fantasy like The Student of Prague had used effects like double exposure and stop-motion, and Paul Wegener had championed the use of cinematic trickery to revitalise Germany's literary tradition of fairy tale. The Swedish director Victor Sjöström made extensive use of effects like superimposition in The Phantom Carriage (1920), a film that Murnau admired.

the call of the Bird of Death

In later films Murnau, with bigger budgets, achieved even more spectacular effects (Mephistopheles takes Faust on a sky-ride around the earth; the City Woman in *Sunrise* conjures up a vision of the big city for the man she is seducing).

titles

Inter-titles irritate a modern audience and Murnau himself moved towards fewer titles in his films, with *The Last Laugh* having only one in the entire film.

Nosferatu has 75 titles. Grau's designs, however, contribute to the texture and atmosphere of the film. This was lost when the film fell into disrepair, but the Photoplay restoration now allows us to see them as they originally appeared.

Besides their visual impact, the titles have a lurid poetry, as when the narrator likens the word 'Nosferatu' to the call of the Bird of Death, and warns of the consequences of uttering it.

Of course, the titles are important as an element in our understanding of the narrative. When Ellen asks Hutter why he 'destroyed the beautiful flowers' the sense of the scene is clearer than in prints which lack the title.

sound

Obviously there are no diegetic sounds – we never hear wolves howl, the wind roar, or Nosferatu's voice – and for a modern audience this can be disconcerting, but it does add to the film's other-worldly atmosphere. And the film does evoke sounds at times – Hutter jumps when the skeleton clock chimes; a cock crows. The shots of the sea have such an insistent rhythm one can almost hear the waves break.

music

Music is enormously important in our enjoyment and understanding of films. In the silent era, films were always accompanied by music, but even when a film had its own score audiences did not always hear it. Cinemas

the accompaniment of all kinds of music

varied in the musical resources they could afford. While a big city cinema could have an orchestra, a small venue might only have a tinny piano.

One can see *Nosferatu* to the accompaniment of all kinds of music from monotonous organ doodles to avant-garde jazz. Music affects one's sense of the rhythm of the narrative, of its dramatic contours, anticipations and echoes. Eureka's DVD release has a modern score using electronic keyboards with some effective percussive sounds (cowbells when Hutter wakes up at the inn, a relentless ticking that suggests fate), but at times is too insistent. James Bernard's score (the Photoplay restoration/BFI DVD) is more traditional, using a full orchestra in a 'romantic' style closer to Erdmann's, and employs melodic themes to represent different characters and moods.

contexts

production history

PRINCIPAL PHOTOGRAPHY

Shooting began in August 1921 and lasted until October. Unlike many of the German films of the period, *Nosferatu* made extensive use of real locations. For the Carpathian mountains, the Upper Tatras (then in Czechoslovakia but now in Poland) were used; the vampire's castle was the thirteenth-century Oravsky Castle near the River Oravia in Slovakia. The Baltic ports of Rostock, Wismar and Lübeck provided the harbour and street scenes of Wisborg; Nosferatu's sinister dwelling, from which he stares forlornly at Ellen's bedroom, was in old salt warehouses at Lübeck on a tributary of the River Elbe. In Luciana Berriatua's fascinating documentary for Spanish Television *The Language of Shadows*, one can see that many of the locations used in the film remain intact. The interior scenes were shot at the Jofa-Atelier in Berlin.

According to Barry Salt, the film was shot partly at 18 frames per second and partly at 20 frames per second (Salt, 1983). Berriatua believes it was filmed at 18 fps.

POST-PRODUCTION

Editing: One of the most striking features of German film-making in the 1920s is that it was common for directors to edit their own films. Given this practice, it is unlikely that Murnau, a notorious perfectionist, entrusted the creative editing decisions to others.

Colour: During the silent era, films were often coloured by painting each frame, or by tinting and toning scenes with stencils and dyes. Colour codes were developed – red for firelight, light amber or yellow for exteriors, dark amber for exteriors, pink for dawn and for romance. Night scenes were shot during the day and tinted blue. Thanks to the restoration work done

a constant stream of press releases

on the film, we can now see the film as it was intended – dawn and dusk scenes are tinted pink, while scenes at night appear blue unless they are candlelit interiors.

Music: An orchestral score was commissioned from composer Hans Erdmann (1887–1948). The musical director of the theatre of Jena in 1919–20, he devoted much of his career to film music, writing scores for at least three sound films (including Fritz Lang's *The Testament of Dr Mabuse*), and edited the journal *Film-Ton-Kunst* (in 1926). The score that Erdmann wrote for *Nosferatu* has not survived as such and scholars have had to guess, from other pieces he wrote with fantastic themes and titles, what the music must have sounded like. In 1927 he co-wrote a *Handbook of Film Music* – this book includes a 'suite fantastico-romantique' with headings that suggest it was the music for *Nosferatu*.

PUBLICITY AND MARKETING

To promote interest in the film while it was in production, Prana issued a constant stream of press releases and articles to German film magazines, as well as holding a press conference at which stills were shown; journalists were invited onto the set.

In *Der Film* (issue 27, 1921) Prana announced that the preparations for *Nosferatu* were over and shooting was about to commence. This was July. In a late August issue (No. 33) of *Der Film*, Prana informed readers that the crew had just returned from shooting exteriors, having obtained 'splendid images of the coast and high seas', and that a second shooting spell was planned in the Balkans and in Asia Minor (the latter never took place). When the interior scenes were being filmed at the Jofa-Atelier, a journalist from *Der Film* (issue 43) was invited to observe:

> On Thursday, in the Jofa Studios, were shot the last scenes of *Nosferatu* … Making up a pleasing composition, some old boats were anchored and the quay was full of bags, barrels, and dockers busied themselves. … In the ghostly light, in the middle of an ink-black night, the scene struck one in an extraordinary way even when one is used to a film shoot. Not far from the sailing boats

was a plane; its engine made its propellor turn and, in the harbour, the sails were soon swelling strongly and boats were floating cheerfully in the breeze. As usual, Murnau is only called upon when a scene is totally ready to be shot; but until then, the artistic director Albin Grau has carefully prepared it in the smallest detail, along psychological and pictorial principles ... Each gesture, each costume (1840 style), each step, each movement is determined with scientific rigour according to the effect it will have on the spectator. Grau and Murnau thus produce a remarkable work of detail without losing sight of the main structure of the work.

This is the scene when sailors search the rat-infested coffins bound for Wisborg. The description suggests how important Grau was in the production of the film.

Impressive 'expressionistic' posters for the film were designed by Grau, one of which featured Nosferatu dwarfing a town and its fleeing inhabitants, his claws slashing the title out of the air, a retinue of flying rats forming a sort of rainbow alongside him.

The issue of *Buhne und Film* (No. 21) which was devoted to the film contained, besides impressive production sketches and stills, a piece by Grau entitled *Vampires* in which he related an experience he claimed to have had during the war. Billeted with an old peasant in Serbia, he and his comrades had heard, gathered around a fire one windy night, a story about a real-life vampire. The peasant's father had, after death, haunted the village as a blood-sucker. When the body was disinterred, officials found no signs of decomposition, but on the contrary rosy cheeks. Only a stake through the heart laid the man to rest for good. Grau saw an official document to corroborate the man's tale. Did he believe this? Was he implying that the film should be read as grounded in reality?

THE PREMIERE

On 4 March 1922 the film premièred in the Marble Hall of the Berlin Zoological Gardens. An elaborate affair which cost more than the film

a bid to suppress the film

itself, the evening began with a spoken prologue inspired by Goethe's *Faust*, followed by a performance from Elisabeth Gruber of the National Opera who danced with a ballet troupe. After the film was screened, there was a Ball which continued late into the night. Berlin's 'glitterati' were there and had an enjoyable time. *Film Kurier* (6 March 1922) reported that 'the guests quickly turned the "symphony of horror" into a delightful symphony of merriment'.

The film was favourably reviewed (see Interpretations).

LAWSUIT

The future of the film, however, was soon in doubt. Florence Stoker, the widow of the author of *Dracula*, got wind of *Nosferatu*'s release and contacted the British Society of Authors in a bid to suppress the film for breach of copyright. Once considered a great 'society beauty' and courted by several famous Victorians, she was now living in genteel poverty and depended on royalties from her husband's writings. Her dogged persistence in pursuing the case led to a German court ruling against Prana in July 1924. Prana meanwhile had gone bankrupt, and on 20 July 1925 the film's new owners (Deutsch Film Produktion) were ordered to destroy the negative and all prints.

CAREER OF THE FILM

Notwithstanding Florence Stoker's apparent success in burying the film, it refused to disappear. In November 1922 a version was seen in Paris and, although no box-office 'smash', was becoming a cult film for Surrealist artists who cited it as a pioneer of poetic cinema.

To Mrs Stoker's dismay, there were even attempts to screen a print in London: a distributor bought the British rights to the film in 1922 and approached the British Board of Film Censors for a certificate; on 11 December the BBFC rejected it. The Board's records do not state a reason. Had it heard of the legal case in Germany? As it was, no one in the British film industry, nor Mrs Stoker, even knew of the application. Three years elapsed before another attempt was made – in 1925 the London Film Society was set up and planned Sunday afternoon screenings; as a club, they didn't need a certificate and announced a showing of *Nosferatu*; Florence Stoker threatened legal action and the plan was cancelled. The Society did, finally, screen it on 16 December 1928 at the New Gallery Kinema in Regent Street, which led to Florence obtaining the right to seize the print; it was allegedly burned in April 1929.

A print only reached America seven years after its Berlin release, being premièred in New York in June 1929 at Greenwich Village's Film Guild Cinema (a venue which later became the home of late-night showings of the *Rocky Horror Picture Show*). By this time, 'talkies' were replacing silent films and it received a lukewarm response from US critics. Mordaunt Hall in the *New York Times* (4 June, 1929) commented that 'Max Schreck's movements are too deliberate to be life-like', while *Variety*, although saying that it was 'skilfully mounted and directed', deplored the 'mis-spotted and poor titling' which 'lends the film more than one confusing moment'. Poor prints were already undermining its impact.

The American screening took place as Universal Studio was planning the first Hollywood version of *Dracula*; inspired by the success of a Broadway adaptation, it was in the middle of negotiations with an irritable Florence Stoker. To remove a potential 'spanner in the works', Universal bought the US print for $400 and took it out of circulation (except to use excerpts of it in a comedy short called *Boo!*).

SURVIVAL AT A PRICE

The film survived but in damaged forms. Prints circulated with missing scenes, mistranslated inter-titles, and no colour tinting.

More confusion was added when a film entitled *The Twelfth Hour* appeared in 1929 – released as an 'artistic adaptation' by Dr Waldemar Roger, it was *Nosferatu* with a new music score, discarded out-takes, and scenes that Wagner had never filmed; a happy ending was engineered by transposing early scenes of the film to the end. The company that had acquired Prana's film on its bankruptcy had not carried out the court order to destroy it. They were trying to make some money out of what they hoped was a more commercial version.

fully colour-tinted and toned

THE RESTORATION

It has taken years of painstaking work in several countries to undo the damage inflicted on the original film. In the 1950s, Lotte Eisner obtained, from his brother Robert, Murnau's copy of the script. This was an invaluable aid in restoration, as well as revealing Murnau's alterations to Galeen's original ideas. She also cleared up confusions caused by *The Twelfth Hour.*

In the mid-1970s, restoration was begun by Enno Patalas of the Munich Film Museum. The museum obtained its first copy in 1976 – a version with German titles that had been shown by the Atlas Distribution Company all through the 1960s. These titles had been translated from English (from a copy in the Museum of Modern Art, New York), which in turn had been translated from French (from a French version that MOMA had acquired). He subsequently used a copy of a 1926 French release and two German copies as well as the print, from the French cinémathèque, of *The Twelfth Hour*, the latter yielding shots from Murnau's script that were missing from the other three versions. All of these copies, however, were in black and white. Patalas was sure that the original was tinted and that it had employed the colour coding of the period.

In 1984, a breakthrough came when an original nitrate print of the first French release was discovered by Luciano Berriatua in the French cinémathèque. Although worn and incomplete, it was fully colour-tinted and toned.

Workers at two film archives (the Munich Filmmuseum and the Bologna Cineteca in Italy) collated all the existing material, recopying it using improved technology developed by Noel Desmet of the Cinémathèque Royale de Belgique. A beautifully restored *Nosferatu* was premièred in 1995 at the Cannes Film Festival (at midnight), and at the Cinema Ritrovaro Festival at Bologna with a live performance of music by Erdmann.

For its première at the London Film Festival, Photoplay Productions, with the support of Channel 4, commissioned a score by James Bernard, which was played live and conducted by Nic Raine. Bernard was an inspired choice, having written music for several Hammer films (beginning with

Murnau was not a 'horror director'

The Quatermass Experiment in 1955 and including its first international success *The Curse of Frankenstein* in 1957).

Channel 4 has broadcast the Photoplay restoration three times, and The British Film Institute released it on DVD in May 2001.

Eureka Video has released DVDs with good picture quality and titles in a flamboyantly Gothic style (although not the original style). They contain all the shots of the Photoplay Restoration but have a modern music score (by Gérard Hourbette and Thierry Zaboitzeff, performed by Art Zoyd); they have no colour tinting, so Nosferatu appears to be carrying his coffin about in broad daylight.

genre

Nosferatu is usually discussed first and foremost in terms of its relationship to the popular sub-genre of vampire movies.

When it was made, the 'vampire film' did not exist. Films had been made with 'vampire' in their titles, but this referred to 'dangerous women' (vamps).

There had been no German vampire film before, but there was a tradition of 'terror tales' (by writers like Hoffmann, author of *The Sandman*, in the late nineteenth century), and a number of films had already begun to develop a cinema of the fantastic. Most important were the films of Paul Wegener (1874–1948); Wegener was an actor/film-maker who realised that film could give new form to German uncanny tales. In *The Student of Prague* (1913) he played a man who sells his soul to the Devil and, using special effects, appeared on screen simultaneously with his evil double. *Nosferatu* was seen by audiences at the time as following in Wegener's footsteps. It was also considered an 'artistic' film, what we now call an 'independent' or 'alternative' film, as well as a film by a promising auteur.

Only in retrospect can we discuss how it compares to later versions of *Dracula* and to vampire films generally. Although he also made a version of *Dr Jekyll and Mr Hyde*, Murnau was not a 'horror director' and when he moved to Hollywood showed no interest in helping to develop the genre.

Hollywood's Dracula talked and had sex appeal

INFLUENCE ON FILM HISTORY

Measuring the impact of a film on film history is difficult. *Nosferatu* is now regarded as a horror 'classic', but it was Universal's *Dracula* that established the vampire film as a commercial proposition, Bela Lugosi's portrayal of the Count being the one that audiences were most familiar with for years to come. Hollywood's Dracula talked and had sex appeal; he was exotic without being too alien; frightening, but not too frightening.

Nosferatu may have been a source for moments in Tod Browning's film (e.g. when Dracula wines and dines his guest in his Hall) – Universal had bought the American print and *Dracula*'s cameraman, Karl Freund, was one of many German craftsmen who moved to Hollywood (he worked with Murnau on *The Last Laugh*) – but the film was closer to the stage play and also, reflecting early problems of sound recording, has a very static quality.

The impact of *Nosferatu* can be seen more clearly in other films. Carl Dreyer's *Vampyre* (1933), for example, emulates the uncanny atmosphere achieved by Murnau, and has an extraordinary sequence of dancing shadows that recalls his use of shadow play. Pauline Kael sees its influence in Ingmar Bergman's *The Magician* (which has a similar coach sequence) and Jean Luc Godard's *Alphaville* (its use of negative). In some modern horror films we see its legacy: Werner Herzog remade *Nosferatu* in 1979 with Bruno Ganz as Hutter, Isabelle Adjani as Ellen and Klaus Kinski as Orlok. Made in colour, and with a powerful soundtrack (combining Wagner and Popul Vuh), it follows the original closely in some respects (with a few moments of shot-for-shot recreation) but also contains interesting departures. A major difference between the two films is in the ending – after Ellen and the vampire die, we discover that Hutter has become a vampire and will perpetuate evil. *Salem's Lot* (Tobe Hooper) has a vampire clearly modelled on Nosferatu, and the German vampire sometimes makes 'guest appearances' in films – in *Scream2*, Casey watches him on late-night TV. Coppola's *Bram Stoker's Dracula* developed the way in which, in *Nosferatu*, the Count's shadow can take on an independent life. Most recently, *The Shadow of the Vampire* (Merhige) employs the premiss that Max Schrèck was a genuine vampire with whom Murnau has made a Faustian pact – sacrificing his leading lady in order to achieve cinematic authenticity.

Explicit inheritance to one side, *Nosferatu* was one of many German films of the early 1920s which impressed film-makers everywhere. Odd camera angles, unusual compositions and chiaroscuro lighting became known as the 'German style', and were widely imitated. Alfred Hitchcock, for example, saw Murnau at work in Germany and, in *The Lodger*, showed what he had learned. Some film historians claim that German influence was a major factor in the development not only of horror films but also of film noir, the name given to a group of gloomy 'thrillers' in the 1940s (*Double Indemnity, Scarlet Street, The Killers* etc.), many of which were directed by German exiles (Wilder, Lang, Siodmak).

GERMAN EXPRESSIONIST FILM

Nosferatu is usually discussed as a classic of 'German Expressionist' cinema. It has often been deemed to belong to a distinctive film movement in 1920s Germany, characterised by an 'excessive' visual style and a focus on the morbid side of human life. Various explanations (usually sociological) are given to account for the movement.

One should appreciate, however, that this is a contested view and not quite as unproblematic as it might appear. To begin with, those who use the term have never agreed which films belong to the 'movement' or what exactly its defining characteristics are. Some writers include *Nosferatu*, while others do not. Barry Salt (1979) argues that only six films are eligible (*Nosferatu* is not among them), Huaco (1965) lists a core of 21 (including *Nosferatu*), while John Barlow (1982) includes almost every film made during the Weimar era as well as films from other historical periods (*Touch of Evil, Night of the Hunter*). If used to describe any form of visual stylisation, or thematic pessimism, 'expressionist' can be applied to a vast range of films.

Using the term has the virtue of drawing attention to the relationships that certainly existed between films and other artistic practices in Germany, and a film like *The Cabinet of Dr Caligari* certainly employed sets and acting styles drawn from Expressionist painting and drama. But one should be

a significant moment in the history of German cinema

careful not to over-simplify – Expressionism in the arts was very diverse (in painting there were Expressionists like Kirchner who retained recognisable imagery, even if exaggerated, while others like Kandinsky pursued complete abstraction), and the films often labelled by the term had as many differences as similarities. All labels can obscure diversity.

In the case of *Nosferatu*, we have seen that its visual style is a complex dialectic of stylisation and **realism**; its use of real locations distances it from a film like *Caligari*. Murnau knew Expressionist artists, but his visual sensibility was more influenced by Romantic painters like Friedrich, and he preferred understatement to exaggeration. Interestingly, Albin Grau, in an essay on film set design, explicitly disavowed Expressionism as an aesthetic, calling its adherents 'extremists' (*Artistic Décor in Cinema*, quoted in Bouvier and Leutrat, 1981).

institutional context

Nosferatu was made at a significant moment in the history of German cinema. In the years that followed the end of the First World War, Germany earned a worldwide reputation for cinematic excellence and innovation. German films won critical acclaim but also scored commercial successes.

Although the First World War had been traumatic for German society, it boosted German cinema. *Nosferatu* was only one of many celebrated films produced in the 1920s and early 30s – *The Cabinet of Dr Caligari*, *Metropolis*, *M*, *Diary of a Lost Girl*, *The Last Laugh*, *The Blue Angel*, *Maidens in Uniform*, *Berlin Symphony of a City*, *The Threepenny Opera*, and many more.

GERMAN CINEMA BEFORE THE FIRST WORLD WAR

Before the war, German pioneers like Oskar Messter contributed to the evolution of film, but its industry was overshadowed by foreign producers. Before 1914, German films barely occupied more than 10% of the domestic market (French films made up 30%, American 25%, Italian 20% and Scandinavian 15%).

The working classes were enthusiastic about film, but the middle classes were dismissive. Newspapers wouldn't review films, theatres tried to prevent actors from taking film work, and powerful pressure groups campaigned against what they saw as the corrupting influence of film. A fierce 'Kino Debate' took place – with the cinema being accused by Conservatives of encouraging crime and lowering moral standards. The more extreme cultural pessimists portrayed cinema as a vampire, draining male energies and seducing women from their 'natural' roles.

GERMAN CINEMA DURING THE FIRST WORLD WAR

The war meant that the demand for films grew enormously, to inform and entertain the nation at a time of stress, but many of its pre-war suppliers were now enemy nations and the Government imposed a ban on imports which, in the case of film, was not removed until 1920. How could the escalating demand be met? Germany's own film-makers would have to fill the gap.

Production expanded dramatically. With less than 30 film production companies in 1913, Germany had well over 200 by 1919. Berlin became the centre of a thriving film industry and attracted talent from all over Central and Eastern Europe.

A major effect of the war was that Governments began to appreciate the role that film could play not only in sustaining morale but also as a weapon of propaganda. Members of Germany's military elite like General Ludendorff felt that decisive action was needed to strengthen German film; with the financial support of the Government and the Deutsche Bank, the High Command initiated, in December 1917, a major merger of leading German companies into a film giant – UFA (Universum Film). Germany now had a **vertically integrated** film company, owning production Studios, distribution networks and cinema chains on a scale comparable to the Hollywood Studios. In fact, UFA's career had only begun when Germany accepted defeat. It soon had a new role – to lead the fight by Germany's expanded film industry to survive the renewed competition from foreign film producers which would accompany peace and a return to normal trade. However, for all its size and influence, UFA did not dominate German film production in the way that Hollywood controlled American cinema.

the German film industry had never been stronger

There were many small companies, like Prana, and this competition encouraged innovation.

POST FIRST WORLD WAR GERMAN CINEMA

Despite the turmoil of the immediate post-war years, the German film industry had never been stronger. Even the country's economic problems favoured its film producers – inflation meant that Germany could produce films at a fraction of the cost possible in rival film-producing nations and sell them at a price that undercut competitors. Widespread unemployment meant that labour and extras were cheap, while the instability of the German currency discouraged foreign film companies from investing in Germany, which delayed competition for its producers.

In 1921, the year that *Nosferatu* was being made, Germany produced 646 films and around 2000 during the decade as a whole. This was more than the rest of Europe combined, and only Hollywood exceeded it (producing around 7000 in the 1920s).

THE 1920 REICH FILM ACT

The Government shaped the cinema of the time by reintroducing film censorship (which had been abolished at the end of the war), and enforcing age restrictions (children under 12 were not allowed into the cinema). More positively, the Act regulated film imports, which offered some protection to German producers when Hollywood began to increase its share of the market. Finally, taxation rules were drawn up so that any cinema owner who showed educational and artistic films was able to claim a reduction in the entertainment levy.

THE GERMAN ART FILM

Some producers wanted to make films that could attract 'upmarket' audiences both in Germany and in export markets. Germany alone wasn't sufficiently large to support a film industry to compete with Hollywood, so success abroad was essential. 'Blockbusters' might be one strategy, but could German films excel in other ways and win over an affluent, educated audience? In February 1920, Berlin witnessed the première of *The Cabinet*

an Expressionist style

of Dr Caligari, a film which convinced many of those who saw it that film had finally become an art.

Made by Decla Bioscop, a company whose top producer was Erich Pommer, a passionate advocate of a European cinema to rival Hollywood, it was written by Hans Janowitz and Carl Mayer; their wartime experiences of unjust authority inspired a tale of an insane doctor who exploits a somnambulist to murder those who offend him. The original idea was changed during production so that the story is revealed, in the film's final scene, to be the delusion of a mental patient.

The film's notoriety owed most to its two central performances (by Werner Krauss as Dr Caligari and Conrad Veidt as his somnambulist Cesare) and to its extraordinary sets. Its art designers (Hermann Warm, Walter Reimann, and Walter Röhrig) chose an Expressionist style. The performers in *Caligari* move through a world that is blatantly artificial, with shadows and menacing shapes painted on weirdly angular sets. Rather than persuading the viewer of the reality of what is seen, the sets could be perceived as projecting a world of insanity or the derangement of its sick narrator. The film demonstrated that cinema need not rely on the photographic reproduction of reality, but could be subjective, artificial, even abstract. *Caligari*'s success encouraged not only its director Robert Wiene (in *Genuine* and *Raskolkinov*), but other film-makers to make artistic films in a fantastic mode. It was these films that acquired the label 'Expressionist'.

social & historical context

Nosferatu was made shortly after Germany's defeat in the First World War. Many accounts of the film claim it reflects this experience in its narrative themes, the vampire being interpreted as representing social fears of the time (see Interpretions). It is difficult to prove such claims since the film makes no explicit reference to contemporary events, being a story of the supernatural set in the 1840s, but if one wants to make such an interpretation some knowledge of the historical background is essential.

living labour is 'bled'

THE FIRST WORLD WAR

A horrific conflict, the war of 1914–18 left a deep scar on a generation of Europeans; technology had transformed blood-letting into slaughter on an industrial scale, and its effects echoed throughout the century.

In Russia Tsarist aristocracy was the first casualty when, in 1917, the Bolsheviks seized power and promised, besides peace, to instigate a new era of classless society. The revolutionaries espoused the ideas of Karl Marx, who had formulated a powerful critique of social exploitation. He often used vampire imagery to describe how the rich and powerful drain life out of working people. In the case of capitalism, he argued that living labour is 'bled' to expand the wealth of those who control society's productive resources, with wars as the consequence of competition between growing capitalist nations for economic power.

Germany also had an authoritarian political system. Despite rapid industrialisation, urbanisation, and the growth of a working class movement, its political system remained undemocratic, dominated by an aristocratic elite headed by Kaiser Wilhelm II. This elite took Germany into war.

THE EFFECTS OF DEFEAT

After losing two million men, defeat came as a shattering blow to the German people and triggered off a dramatic chain of events, which resulted in the formation of Germany's first democracy – the Weimar Republic (1919–33).

As the reality of defeat hit home, Germany's elites were put on the defensive. The Allied Governments would not negotiate with an undemocratic Germany and large numbers of German workers, soldiers and sailors began, through strikes and mutinies, to demonstrate their anger at what had happened. Was Germany about to follow Russia into revolution? On 28 October 1918, sailors at Kiel refused to obey orders and subsequently took over the town; in November workers and soldiers began to set up organs of popular power across the country. Facing rebellion, the Kaiser abdicated and a Republic was declared.

A crucial role now fell into the hands of the leading workers' party, the Social Democratic Party. The SPD found itself in a position to help construct a democratic system. Would the SPD play the part that the Bolsheviks had assumed in Russia?

FATAL COMPROMISE

The SPD was, however, a moderate party in practice. Its leaders believed in gradual change and attempted to steer Germany towards parliamentary democracy. There would be reforms but no attempt to construct a revolutionary new society.

Meanwhile they had to sue for peace and sent a delegation to meet the Allied leaders. The nation reeled when it heard the vindictive terms of the Versailles Treaty. The Allied leaders wanted to see a democratic Germany, but also had to satisfy their electorates' thirst for revenge. The nation lost land and raw materials, faced gigantic reparations payments to reimburse the Allies for war damage, and had to dramatically reduce its armed forces. Germany also had to accept blame for the war. The treaty was felt by Germans to be unjust and, when it added to the country's huge economic problems, was perceived to be sucking the life out of the nation. Could this have added to the resonance of the idea of vampirism?

INTERNAL CONFLICT

While peace terms were being agreed, Germany's new leaders had to deal with explosive domestic unrest. For two years, there was a wave of attempts, principally in industrial areas, to create 'Red Republics' through force of arms. The director Fritz Lang recalled, years later, driving to work on his first film, having to negotiate barricades and street fighting. The revolutionaries were, however, disunited over tactics, failed to win sufficient support, and their use of force only rallied the middle classes, who feared 'Bolshevik anarchy', in support of bloody suppression. The SPD felt it had no choice but to ask army officers and right-wing volunteers (*Freikorps*) to quell the rebellions. The Weimar Republic survived, but at the cost of relying on the most conservative sections of German society, on people who resented the collapse of the monarchy, and who only accepted the democratic Government as a lesser of evils. This proved fatal in the long run.

The new Government faced both left-wing and right-wing hostility, evident when, in March 1920, the radical Right staged a coup – the Kapp Putsch – in an attempt to destroy the fledgling Republic.

There were no more coup attempts in 1921 and 1922, but there was a series of political murders, by right-wing groups, of leading politicians. Does *Nosferatu* encode middle class insecurities? Could the climate of conspiracy and political polarisation be what lay behind those films that featured diabolical masterminds and characters psychologically divided against themselves?

DISEASE

To add to Germany's sufferings was an outbreak of Spanish influenza which swept across Europe in the winter of 1919/20, and probably killed as many civilians as the war. The theme of contagion in *Nosferatu* had immediate resonance.

ANTI-SEMITISM

Conservatives blamed Jews for the nation's misery. This was irrational and unjust, since many Jews had fought in the German army and formed a loyal minority of the population, but the myth developed (exploited by the Nazis) that Germany had been 'stabbed in the back' by Jews. Since some of the Communist leaders and Weimar politicians were Jewish, a huge conspiracy was imagined and became a central theme in right-wing propaganda and iconography. When Jews from Eastern Europe migrated into Germany, they became a convenient scapegoat. It was common in racist literature to associate Jews with rats and even to depict them as vampires. As we will see, some film critics have alleged that *Nosferatu* evoked a fear of Jewish 'contagion'.

WOMEN IN WEIMAR

The Weimar era was a time of stress for all social groups faced with the impact of modernisation and the traumatic after-effects of war, but it was

the liberated 'new woman'

especially contradictory for women, who experienced novel opportunities but also new pressures and dilemmas.

Women had made a major contribution to the war effort, but in exposing them to types of work that had been male preserves it destabilised gender relations. After the conflict was over, men expected a return to traditional roles, but for many women this was impossible since they had lost their husbands. Although women found work in new occupations (secretarial, welfare, nursing etc.), they were worse paid than men and had to combine work with housework and childcare.

The new democracy gave women the vote, but they remained second class citizens. Some were able to take advantage of greater opportunities and the liberated 'new woman' became a popular media icon. This was more myth than reality, however, and provoked a 'moral panic' among Conservatives about the decline of the family, which added to pressures on women to conform.

Except for a few radical feminists, many women, like men, assumed that women and men belonged to separate spheres and that a woman's basic role was to be motherly and self-sacrificing. Is the ending of *Nosferatu*, in which Ellen consents to give up her own life to save her husband and the town, intended to reinforce traditional values? Or does her independent action shame the men in the community who are unable to resist the threat?

HOMOSEXUALS IN WEIMAR

One social group that did not gain legal rights with the establishment of democracy was the German gay community. The infamous Paragraph 175 of the nineteenth-century Criminal Code remained in place, which made homosexual activity illegal for men and subject to harsh punishment (lesbianism was not recognised in law). During the Weimar era, Conservative politicians even tried to make the law more severe, arguing that homosexuality would lead to the degeneration of the nation. The Nazis described homosexuality as an 'evil lust of the Jewish soul' (quoted in Stumke, 1996).

a lively gay and lesbian subculture

Despite legal hostility, there was a lively gay and lesbian subculture in Germany, particularly in Berlin, to which many members of the film and artistic community belonged, including Murnau, the director of *Nosferatu*. Some discussions of the film read it as a coded statement about the alienation felt by those labelled 'deviant'.

interpretations

Since the moment of its release, *Nosferatu* has provoked very different interpretations. Seen as morbid and reactionary by some, others have discerned progressive and subversive qualities within it. It has been called the most beautiful film ever made (by the French Surrealist poet Robert Desnos), while several commentators claim it articulates a sinister ideology.

It has been 'read' as:

■ a coded portrait of its director's psychosexual identity
■ a metaphor for the social and political turmoil in Germany at the time
■ a complex meditation on the dynamics of human desire
■ an essay on the fear of death and disease
■ being about the nature of cinema itself

as well as combinations of all of these.

These different interpretations partly reflect the varied perspectives and agendas of their proponents as well as illustrating the heterogeneity of approaches to the study of film in general. A survey of the readings of *Nosferatu* gives one a sense of how film theories have changed over time, as well, perhaps, of the pitfalls of interpretation.

The diversity of interpretations also reflects the nature of the film itself. Like Hitchcock's *The Birds*, it invites interpretive wheels to spin. An enigmatic film, its curious history has added to its elusive nature. It is highly ambiguous, full of allusions and echoes. Poetic rather than prosaic, each image ricochets off other images. Documentary realism is combined

highly ambiguous, full of allusions and echoes

with an atmosphere of the uncanny. At times one isn't sure whether one is meant to be afraid or to laugh. Like its eponymous 'hero', it seems substantial one minute and goes up in a puff of smoke the next.

Murnau never discussed *Nosferatu* and was not a theorist of cinema. We can only infer his social and political outlook from his films – which suggest he had fairly conventional, broadly liberal views: in *The Burning Earth* the hero comes to repent, after his wife has committed suicide, that he had put financial gain before family values; *The Last Laugh* sympathises with the doorman of a big hotel when his precious uniform is taken from him by a heartless manager and he is reduced to lavatory attendant. *The Finances of the Grand Duke* pits an affable aristocrat against an unlikely band of pantomime revolutionaries and a predatory businessman intent on turning the kingdom into odorous sulphur mines. In *Satanas*, a film in three episodes (of which only fragments exist today), one of the men who fails the test of genuine virtue is a left-wing revolutionary leader. Women, in Murnau's films, range from noble, motherly figures (e.g. in *Phantom*) to shrewish gossips (in *The Last Laugh*, the doorman's humiliation causes delight among his female neighbours) and 'femmes fatales' (the 'City Woman' in *Sunrise*, who encourages the 'Man' to murder his wife).

We will never know what he thought he had achieved in *Nosferatu*, or even whether he attached personal importance to it. He was allegedly superstitious and consulted astrologers – did he believe in supernatural evil? Or perhaps the film was an astute career move, a 'calling card' to the industry that would advertise his talents, rather than anything of deep personal meaning? And what of Galeen and Grau's contributions?

initial responses

When the film was first released most reviews were positive, some being highly complimentary. *Lichtbild-Buhne* (No. 11) called it a 'masterpiece' while *Der Film* (No. 11) used the word 'masterstroke'. *Das Tagebuch* (18 March 1922) called Murnau 'exceptional' and thought that his film had 'tenderness and poetry'. The *Vossische Zeitung* (No. 135, 7 March 1922) enthused:

initial responses

Henrik Galeen's *Nosferatu* could come out of Wegener's workshop. Murnau has created each picture carefully. The castle of horror, the house of Nosferatu, are fantastic achievements. *Nosferatu* is played by a debut actor: Max Schreck. His appearance is gloomy, deathly pale with devils' claws. Refreshing in all that tragic darkness: Gustav von Wangenheim ... Greta Schroeder, his wife, stunningly beautiful on the big screen.

Most critics praised its pictorial qualities and situated the film in the tradition of fantastic literature, evoking the names of Edgar Allan Poe and Hoffmann. *Der Film* (No. 42, 16 October 1921) suggested that Nosferatu symbolises death and fate.

Bela Balazs, one of the first great theorists of film, saw it in Austria and was impressed by how the film re-invigorated his sense of the natural world and of 'the hitherto neglected mysteries of nature'; he praised its uncanny atmosphere, commenting that the film 'conveyed an icy wind reaching us from the "other side of the world"' (quoted in Arnold, 2000).

Even before its release, Prana itself had attempted to shape critical reaction by emphasising its roots in the fantastic genre.

It is clear from the magazine coverage, some of which depended heavily on Prana's statements, that the film targeted an intellectual audience. In the issue of *Buhne und Film* devoted to the film (No. 19, 1921) one of the articles was entitled *The film of intellectuals*. Unsigned and accompanied by two drawings by Grau, it was possibly his or Galeen's manifesto. It said that the film was 'something out of the ordinary' and went on to call for a new cinema in opposition to entertainment cinema.

The strangest, and in some ways the most interesting piece to appear before the film's release was a curious article in Issue 21 of *Buhne und Film* headed 'erotico-occult-spirito-metaphysical film'! This carried the by-line 'Fritz Albrecht', but one wonders if it wasn't another Prana pseudonym. The text, written like a prose poem and obviously designed to 'hype' the film, describes how everyone is becoming thrilled and infatuated by Nosferatu's arrival, as though he were a glamorous new movie star. The author, at one point, says that Lola, a young woman about town, cannot contain her

a sad symptom of the war

excitement – 'I'm already completely crazy about Nosferatu', she says. Tongue in cheek, the piece has a humorous tone that is usually missing from discussions of the film.

The only hostile response to *Nosferatu* came from a socialist newspaper *Leipziger Volkszeitung* (15 March 1922), which accused the film of being an 'ideal means to turn workers away from any excessive and undesirable political activity'. It condemned the film's 'occultism' as a sad symptom of the war, but more importantly as a 'supernatural fog' through which workers would be 'unable to see concrete reality any longer' (quoted in Arnold, 2000). The article added that the industrialists who were funding Prana were only concerned to mystify the working class.

This review was unusual in linking it to the war and gives a brief glimpse of important debates that would occupy German intellectuals and political activists throughout the decade – about the role of the artist in political conflict and about the ideological impact of cinema. Many on the German Left were unsympathetic to artistic experiments that lacked overt social content, and were suspicious of the German film industry's output as a whole – the same year that *Nosferatu* was released also saw the première of *Fridericus Rex*, a hugely popular historical blockbuster from the huge UFA Studio; German Socialists and Communists were incensed by what they perceived as a glorification of German militarism and aristocracy.

In a reply to *Leipziger Volkszeitung*'s attack, another magazine, *Film-Holle* (April 1922), derided its lack of a sense of humour and naïveté about the film business. Did the socialist journal believe that audiences were stupid? Or that the financial backers of the film were really that clever? *Film-Holle* suggested that the investors might have found better ways to spend their money!

THE SURREALIST RESPONSE

One of the most important early responses to the film, which did an enormous amount to build its artistic reputation, was an enthusiastic reaction from the French Surrealists in the late 1920s and 30s. A movement of poets and painters, Surrealism was not only an artistic approach, characterised by strange, dream-like imagery, but a radical philosophy of life in which art was a way of liberating individuals and society. The Surrealists wanted to get in contact with the deepest recesses of the mind, to free the imagination. For them, *Nosferatu* was proof that film could participate in their project to escape the prison of mundane life and to create a realm of the 'marvellous'. It was, in their view, a liberating film. The moment when Hutter crosses the bridge to meet the vampire was one of their most treasured scenes, which they saw as a transition from the real to the 'surreal' (they fondly quoted the mistranslated French subtitle 'As he crossed the bridge, the phantoms came to meet him'). André Breton, the leading figure within French Surrealism, wrote about *Nosferatu* in his books *Communicating Vessels* and *Surrealism and Painting*, comparing it to the eerie work of Italian painter Giorgio di Chirico. The poet Robert Desnos described it as the most beautiful film he had ever seen, using 'beauty' in its surrealist sense as something 'convulsive' (life-changing).

Mainstream French critics, it must be said, took little notice of the film but, when they did, praised its photography and related it to 'grand guignol'. In Paris the Grand Guignol was a theatre specialising in spooky and horrific spectacles. *Export-Film* (No. 9, August 1922) commented 'one will shudder when watching *Nosferatu* and one will think about it at night' while *Le Petit Journal* (3 November 1922) begged to disagree – 'bad grand guignol, grand guignol for babies'.

THE AMERICAN RESPONSE

Nosferatu only reached New York in 1929. Fears of a German invasion of the US market, provoked by *Passion* and *The Cabinet of Dr Caligari* (which even led to a minor anti-German riot in Los Angeles), had petered out and many German directors were working in Hollywood. Murnau's *Sunrise*, made for Fox, had been a critical success if not a commercial one, and his vampire film was seen in this context. *Variety*'s review (25 December 1929) described it as 'a shivery melodrama spilling ghostlike impossibilities from beginning to end'; Murnau received credit as 'a master artisan demonstrating not only a knowledge of the subtler side of directing but in photography', while Max Schreck was praised as 'an able pantomimist ...

his make-up suggesting everything that's goose pimply. He did his worst on every occasion – which was good'. No mention here of German psychology or social events. As a silent film it was now an oddity.

THE FILM CANON

How do films become famous? Behind reputations lies a history of audience and critical reactions, responses that are themselves based on shifting ideas of what makes a 'good' and 'important' film. From this process, a canon emerges – a set of films felt to be of special significance. One can track the broad sweep of canonic construction in the major film histories that have been written; one of the first was *The Film Till Now* (1930), an impressive volume by Paul Rotha. Republished in 1949, this became a 'bible' for film lovers for decades. Rotha was a left-leaning documentary film-maker with a strong belief in the social role of cinema, but who also wanted to see film develop artistically. He had high praise for the German cinema of the 1920s, particularly for *The Cabinet of Dr Caligari* ('the first attempt at the expression of a creative mind in the new medium of cinematography'), but *Nosferatu* also received some compliments (and one photograph):

> ... possibly crude in its melodramatic acting, but nevertheless it contained much of considerable interest. There was a very definite feeling for camera angles in the establishment of a macabre mood, and effective use was made of projected negative and one turn/one picture camera devices for the suggestion of eeriness. Fritz Arno Wagner's camerawork was notably good, particularly a sense of frightened horses in the twilight and the close-ups of the architecture of the Count's castle.
>
> *Rotha, 1949, p. 278*

What is interesting about the vast majority of discussions of *Nosferatu* and German cinema before the Second World War is that it was *not* common to see the films as expressions of the 'German soul' and even less of German political developments. German films were seen as 'heavy' and 'slow', for example, in American reviews, but linking this to national character was a journalistic cliché and one that ignored inconvenient evidence (in the case of Lubitsch) by attributing wit and pace to the director. Most commentators were impressed by the inventiveness and technical brilliance of films like *The Last Laugh*. Only the *Leipziger Volkszeitung*'s review of *Nosferatu* had seen a political plot to distract the working class. Most critics saw it and the films that resembled it as cleverly made fantasies; if their political thrust was considered, which was rare (Kurtz, 1926), they were seen as protests against bourgeois complacency rather than as conservative.

post-war readings

It was in the immediate post-war period that some interpretations of pre-war German films took on a darker tone.

Weimar democracy had been destroyed by Hitler. After the war, and with the full realisation of what had happened in the concentration camps, interest in Weimar Germany revived and took on new significance. For some it was a 'golden age' of democratic experiment and cultural innovation cruelly snuffed out by the Nazis, a period of great achievement in the arts from which we can still learn. For others, however, particularly in the shadow of Germany's shame, there was a desire to understand why Weimar had failed and whether it had not contained the seeds of its own destruction.

siegfried kracauer

It was in this context that Siegfried Kracauer (1899–1966) worked; his writings had an enormous impact on the way that German films from the 1920s and early 30s were interpreted for decades to come. Few writers on film have so dominated their chosen field of film scholarship.

Kracauer had been a cultural critic in Germany and an associate of the 'Frankfurt School' of radical social scientists. He was fascinated by the impact of modernisation and believed that one could best read shifts in society and popular consciousness through everyday activities and enthusiasms like movie-going. In the *Frankfurter Zeitung* he published a

films are expressions of social attitudes

series of articles on a wide range of phenomena from hotel lobbies and dance crazes to the latest films (later published in *The Mass Ornament*). He was critical of escapist films – in an essay he entitled *The Little Shopgirls Go to the Movies*, he analysed a range of popular films for the ways in which they exploited young women's fantasies of romance and wealth. He wrote:

> since it is in the interest of the propertied classes to maintain society as it is, they must prevent others from thinking about that society.
>
> *Kracauer, 1995, p. 296*

When Hitler came to power Kracauer moved to America and, in 1947, published a major study of Weimar cinema – *From Caligari to Hitler*. In this book, he argued that films are expressions of social attitudes. He suggested that cinema is an especially good indicator of a society's preoccupations because it is a collaborative activity seeking popular approval.

He then applied this to the cinema of the Weimar period, claiming that it encoded disturbing ideas and attitudes, widespread in the German nation, which contributed to the success of Nazism. As the title of his book implied, *The Cabinet of Dr Caligari* helped make the rise of Hitler possible. Films had both reflected and reinforced sentiments in the German people that paved the way for evil.

Characters like Caligari and Nosferatu were, in Kracauer's optic, figures of tyranny who fascinated Germans, particularly the beleaguered middle and lower middle classes whose savings and incomes were destroyed by inflation (acting like a vampire), but also from whom they saw no alternative except chaos and anarchy. Such films, he proposed, embodied a fatalism and a retreat from reality that made Nazism inevitable. Every feature of the films he discussed, from their artificial sets to their sadistic plots, pointed to this dreadful conclusion. He saw the prevalence of 'doubles' in these films as an expression of how Germany's middle class was mentally divided – resentful of the aristocratic elite, but afraid to ally themselves with the working class. The fact that many of the films were made in Studios was, he said, symptomatic of a desire to escape from

'an exercise in xenophobia'

Germany's social and economic crisis. In the case of *Nosferatu*, he saw the ending as a wish-fulfilment fantasy – the only escape from tyranny could come from a miracle rather than the result of political action.

sociological readings

KRACAUER'S LEGACY

Kracauer's interpretation proved hugely influential, and many writers have followed his lead in seeing the German films of the Weimar era as dark anticipations of horrors to come. The films are grouped together, usually under the category 'German Expressionist film', and then a direct link is discerned between the themes that all of the films allegedly share and the 'zeitgeist' (spirit of the times) in 1920's Germany. George Huaco read *Nosferatu* in terms of social class conflict, with 'a final duel between bourgeois housewife and evil aristocratic vampire' which, he argued, translates to the screen the 'destructive impact of inflation on the middle class'. He added that the films' conservative ideology reflected the fact that the film-makers were all from middle class backgrounds, which he assumes would make them politically conservative (Huaco, 1965). John Barlow, in *German Expressionist Film*, interprets *Nosferatu* as 'an exercise in xenophobia' (Barlow, 1982). Ken Gelder writes that 'it is difficult *not* to see this German film as anti-Semitic' and 'perhaps Ellen *does* come to represent the 'German soul' here, at the mercy of the property-acquiring Jew-vampire' (Gelder, 1994).

However, one can adopt a sociological perspective to films without endorsing these analyses. Many important writers on German film history today, like Thomas Elsaesser, argue that Kracauer's work, for all its brilliance, had many weaknesses and has regrettably over-shadowed alternative views.

Critics of Kracauer argue that he was highly selective in the films he discussed, and interpreted them in a way that was ultimately circular – in *From Caligari to Hitler*, the only proof he offered that the dispositions of the German people were as he described them was in the films he wanted to explain in their terms. His discussion of individual films was brief and

sociological readings interpretations

usually concentrated on the plot and the themes. Kracauer never allowed for the possibility that a film might have an alternative meaning to the one he relentlessly pursued, or that audiences might read films in different ways. For all his sophistication, he often seemed to subscribe to a simplistic view of the effects of a film on a spectator. Weren't there other overwhelming reasons for the success of Nazism? As Elsaesser comments, the neatness of the fit he found between films and society was due to the fact that his view of how Germany turned to Hitler was like the plot of a film – with a principal protagonist ('psychological dispositions') rather than a complex historical account that would include many factors (the way Germany became a nation, European power politics, the economic crisis of 1929, the role of the Universities etc.). In addition, many of the most popular films in Germany were Hollywood films, which he doesn't discuss.

A major problem with the sociological analyses quoted is that they assert interpretations without empirical evidence of audience responses and ignore recorded reactions (by critics at the time, other writers etc.) which fail to endorse the imputed meaning. Huaco's account is very mechanistic, with crude thumbnail sketches of the films and a dubious assumption that one can deduce political orientation simply from social background (many leading German revolutionaries were 'middle class').

In *Fifty Years of German Cinema* (1947), H.H. Wollenberg warned against exaggerating the importance of the films that Kracauer and most of these discussions focus upon. Wollenberg, who had been the editor of *Lichtbild Buhne* in the 1920s, pointed out that films like *The Cabinet of Dr Caligari* and *Nosferatu* only formed a tiny proportion of Weimar films and were targeted at an intellectual elite rather than the German public as a whole. The films enjoyed by most Germans were romantic comedies, crime thrillers and historical films.

IS NOSFERATU ANTI-SEMITIC?

To read anti-Semitism in *Nosferatu* is to claim that the film is a work of 'evil genius' like Leni Riefenstahl's hymn of praise to Hitler in *The Triumph of the Will*, or *Birth of a Nation* by D.W. Griffith with its racial stereotypes of black Americans – artistically impressive, but deplorable in content. Anti-Semitism was certainly a powerful current in German culture, as it was throughout Europe, and Stoker's *Dracula* has been interpreted as playing on fears of immigration in Victorian England. Jews were associated with plague in the Middle Ages and with the defeat of Germany in the First World War. French racists in the 1920s regularly compared Jews to vampires. Under Nazism, some overtly anti-Semitic films were made. However, Murnau was no political radical, and we have no reason to believe that he was anti-Semitic; the closest friend of his youth, Hans Ehrenbaum-Degele was Jewish and, after his death, Murnau was virtually adopted by Degele's mother, living in a family villa until he finally left Germany in 1926. As we have seen, many of the people who worked on the film were politically radical; Granach was Jewish and Eisner claims that Murnau defended him, when they were both at Reinhardt's school, from anti-Semitic insults. If one examines Galeen's script one discovers there was an 'old Jew' innkeeper, yet he doesn't appear in the film. Nosferatu's hooked nose might be seen as a give-away, but if one examines the racist representations of Jews at the time (wispy beards, thick lips, a kaftan etc.) the vampire does not closely conform. And doesn't the film seem to show some sympathy for the outcast vampire towards the end?

We have no evidence that audiences at the time perceived it to be xenophobic. Lubitsch and other members of the Jewish film community were at the première and there is no record of them being offended by the film. Even Kracauer, a Jewish intellectual highly critical of Weimar films, did not see *Nosferatu* in these terms.

DID FANTASTIC FILMS PAVE THE WAY FOR NAZISM?

Underlying discussions like Kracauer's is the assumption that Nazism succeeded through making appeals to the irrational, and that the 'terror films' of the 1920s were a morbid symptom and contributory cause of a nation's retreat from reason. This view collapses, however, if one agrees with the argument of a historian like William Brustein who, in *The Logic of Evil*, argues that Nazism succeeded because, given the circumstances of the time and the apparent failures of democracy, it appeared to wide sections of the German population as a rational solution to their concrete economic

the genre had to reflect contemporary society

and political problems. Rather than torchlit parades and anti-Semitism, it was principally material self-interest that motivated the German public to opt for Hitler (Brustein, 1996).

It is worth noting that, for the Nazis, modernist art like Expressionism was 'degenerate' ('entartete kunst'), the product of Jews and Bolsheviks. Hitler admired some of the films made in the 1920s, like Fritz Lang's *Siegfried* (Lang was invited to head the industry under the Nazis, but fled the next day), but Nazi tastes favoured popular genres and an optimistic realism rather than films with stylised elements and gloomy plots.

A SOCIAL METAPHOR?

Interpreting *Nosferatu*, or any film, as a social and political metaphor is a valid approach. What is problematic are simplistic 'one liners' that ignore the complexity of films, disregard the mediating factors that shape them, and make mechanistic connections to crude notions of 'society'. Film analyses that wish to 'read' films sociologically must show respect for the complexity of history.

The war and its aftermath may have informed the film. Death and disease, social instability and disrupted relationships were rife. Did Galeen adapt the novel in the way that he did because of a feeling that Western rationality had failed in the trenches of France? He wrote, in an essay on the fantastic film, that the genre had to reflect contemporary society. The streets and hospitals of Berlin must have contained figures as shocking as Orlok, with ruined faces and near-death looks. Vampirism can represent all kinds of social exploitation. Marx used the figure of the vampire to dramatise exploitation – why not interpret *Nosferatu* as a critical rather than conservative metaphor, by men who had fought in the war and lived through the chaos of the immediate post-war years, of how humanity had been bled dry by war and an aristocratic military elite? Nosferatu is after all a Count, and his victims are members of the middle and working classes.

One of the problems with many of the sociological accounts is that they employ too simple a model of the relationship between film and society – ignoring the differences between films, neglecting social diversity (by focusing exclusively on class), and then seeing the link as one of reflection.

Barry Salt (Salt, 1979), has been scathing about lazy accounts of film styles which see a unified movement where none existed. Patrice Petro has brought a feminist perspective to the debate (Petro, 1989), pointing out that gender has been neglected – yet women were an important part of the audience, as were other social groups (like the young), who found cinema a more accessible medium than older arts, and many films clearly address gender issues. Petro has not analysed *Nosferatu*, but Ellen's self-sacrifice could be interpreted in relation to debates about a woman's role – the idea that it was noble for a woman to sacrifice herself to save a male protagonist has a long history in Western literature; Jo Ann Collier argues (1998) that Murnau's films can be seen as re-workings of Wagner's operas, with *Nosferatu* resembling *The Flying Dutchman* in its narrative of female self-sacrifice (she traces a line of descent through Reinhardt).

Elsaesser has argued that when discussing the relationship of films to society we should not neglect the film-makers themselves as a social group and their position as media professionals negotiating a changing marketplace. In the case of films of fantasy, one can see how they might have appealed to particular social groups (Elsaesser argues that the lower middle class fantasised about social mobility because it could not realistically attain it), but they also met the needs of directors like Murnau who wanted to give cinema a more artistic and intellectual status as well as to show off their technical ingenuity.

lotte eisner & art history

The other great post-war writer on German cinema was another German Jewish exile like Kracauer. Eisner worked at the French Cinématheque, whose charismatic founder Henri Langlois was preserving film history as well as inspiring the French 'New Wave' of directors (Godard, Truffaut etc.). She took an art historical view of Weimar cinema and, unlike Kracauer, appreciated the films for their visual complexity and for their intertextuality (links to theatre, literature etc.). She wrote an invaluable study of the period – *The Haunted Screen* – and books on two of its key directors, Murnau and Lang. Her biography of Murnau, upon which anyone interested in the director heavily depends, was based on an intimate

echoes of paintings and plays

knowledge of his films and interviews with many of those who knew and worked with him. She saw him as a 'genius' and she played a key role in advancing his status as *auteur*.

Eisner placed Germany's 'great age of cinema' in the context of Expressionism (which she characterised as a subjectivist approach to art), but placed this in the broader tradition of German Romanticism. She also emphasised the role of Max Reinhardt, whose staging and use of lighting had, she felt, been a major influence but which had been unjustly unrecognised. Unlike Kracauer, who discussed films almost exclusively in terms of plot and theme, Eisner discussed the texture of the films, their lighting, compositions, their echoes of paintings and plays. In the case of *Nosferatu* she wrote rhapsodically about its visual beauty, its use of shadow and real landscape as well as linking its narrative to Romantic writers like Novalis and Schlegel. She speculated on the role that his homosexuality might have played in the film – perhaps his sense of being an outsider affected his choice of stories and themes? Did his tendency to be indirect and allusive derive from his enforced silence about his sexuality?

Where Eisner seemed to echo Kracauer was when, in several places, she invoked the tortured 'German soul' and an alleged 'Nordic' propensity for gloom and despair as explanatory factors. Had the First World War, she wondered, revived a much deeper disposition in Germans to brood on life and death. She didn't see this so much in terms of political conservatism – it was more a question of an existential anguish at the mysteries of mortality and rifts in the human mind.

psychological readings

Some commentators on *Nosferatu* have adopted an approach that de-emphasises social and historical factors, interpreting it psychologically:

Eisner made a few tentative suggestions about Murnau's attraction for stories that revolve around love, loss and the possibility of redemption. Many of his films feature a couple whose relationship is challenged by a third party who 'haunts' them and threatens to destroy their love. In *Nosferatu*, it is the vampire, in *Tabu* a priest, who prevents two young

Nosferatu as the 'Id'

lovers from remaining together. Was Murnau drawn to such themes because of the death of Ehrenbaum-Degele and his frustrated search for personal happiness? Was Murnau's sexual orientation a factor in his films? Unable to reveal himself openly, did his films allow him a coded form of expression?

One of the few extended discussions of *Nosferatu* from a psychological rather than sociological perspective was one by Robin Wood (1970). Wood interprets *Nosferatu* as, together with *Sunrise* and *Tabu*, forming a 'single complex text', which features 'a heterosexual couple threatened by a sinister, usually male, figure'.

Wood argues that *Nosferatu* is 'one of cinema's finest embodiments of ... the Descent Myth', which he adds is 'one of those universal myths that seem fundamental to human experience'. The myth narrates the experience of characters who journey from innocence to a 'terrible underlying reality' which either destroys them or which leaves them wiser. He cites as an example the Greek legend of Persephone, who was abducted by Pluto and taken to the Underworld. She was picking flowers in a spring meadow before her kidnap, just as Hutter picks flowers for Ellen in the opening scene of *Nosferatu*. The couple live in a domestic Eden before Hutter's descent into the evil realm of the vampire.

Nosferatu, Wood says, is the dark side of nature – he comes out of a burrow and is associated with rats. Knock, his agent, is like a monkey when he evades the townsfolk. Although he doesn't discuss Freud, the influence of psychoanalysis is present in Wood's discussion when he refers to Nosferatu as the 'Id', the unconscious side of human beings. He interprets the arches in the film as invoking the forces of repression that try but fail to contain the 'under-nature' of mankind.

For Wood, the characters in *Nosferatu* are 'archetypes', representing fundamental features of human psychology. The film, then, enacts a story with a timeless appeal because it addresses the divided nature of human beings and their need to reintegrate their rational and sexual sides. It is therapeutic for us to consume such narratives.

Wood's essay was originally published in *Film Comment* but reappeared in a set of papers about the Horror Film (Wood, 1979) which included an elaboration of his ideas from a political perspective – capitalist society depends on sexual repression, and the value of horror films is that they involve a 'return of the repressed', which can be a potentially liberating experience.

psychoanalytical readings

In recent years, Film Studies has seen the use of ideas drawn from psychoanalysis. Despite disputes about whether psychoanalysis is scientific or not, some theorists have embraced it as a way to interpret films and our emotional responses to them in terms of psychic conflicts as outlined by Sigmund Freud (1856–1939). These dynamics have a strong sexual dimension and are seen as the result of the drama involved in making the transition from being a baby, dominated by instinctual needs, to an adult individual who has to negotiate social reality.

For Freud, our conscious minds and everyday behaviour are only a 'surface' we have developed in order to fit into society. This is achieved through a process of repressing sexual desires which never wholly succeeds and that can, in some circumstances, make us ill. In dreams and myths, in slips we make and in mental illness, Freud saw the activity of an Unconscious attempting to express itself. What shocked his contemporaries was his emphasis on the importance of sexuality in childhood development – he suggested that a baby's sexuality is 'polymorphous', neither heterosexual nor homosexual but multi-directional. Only gradually does a child direct its sexuality. Freud suggested a fundamental scenario of human maturation – every child, he claimed, passes through a stage of intense sexual feelings towards parents with boys desiring their mothers and girls desiring their fathers. To mature, a boy has to renounce his desire for his mother after coming to terms with a fantasised fear of castration at the hands of his father (the Oedipus Complex). A girl, on the other hand (and controversy followed what many have seen as Freud's misogyny), has to accept that she is already 'castrated' and will only 'win' a penis from a future male partner other than her father (the Electra Complex). Since nothing goes smoothly, even 'healthy adults' bear the psychic scars of these experiences and can revert to earlier stages of desire and fear. Films, psychoanalytic critics argue, are similar to dream experiences (we are in a dark room, our defences are relaxed) in that they allow us to enjoy fantasies and work through anxieties that normal consciousness rejects.

Freud felt that evidence for his theories lay not only in clinical experience with patients, but also in art – how can one explain the bizarre myths and legends that human beings have created? Why did someone imagine the story of Oedipus, a young man who murders his father and marries his mother before blinding himself when he realises what he has done? Or fairy tales full of wicked stepmothers and little girls endangered by wolves? Are these 'just stories' or are they expressions of psychic and sexual conflicts within the human heart?

For some critics, Freud's ideas have seemed useful when considering a genre like horror – how can anyone derive enjoyment from tales of vampires and werewolves? It seems perverse unless, they say, they satisfy perversities in us. Don't horror films 'blow the whistle' on things we are afraid of but secretly desire? Instead of seeing vampires as social metaphors, aren't they better explained by what is 'irrational' within us? On this view, the horror genre and films like *Nosferatu* are 'dream screens' on which are projected not only rational fears (for example, of disease), but also our repressed desires.

On this view, then, *Nosferatu* is a psychosexual drama in which, as Robert Sklar puts it:

> the tryst between Ellen and Nosferatu appears a fulfilment of each one's desire and a tragic end for both.
>
> *Film: An International History of the Medium, Sklar, 1993*

Is Nosferatu a 'return of the repressed'? Is he, in some sense, Hutter's 'double', his 'dark side', and the answer to Ellen's frustrated desire? Tales of horror and fantasy often feature 'doubles (Jekyll and Hyde, men who become werewolves at full moon etc.) and this may be interpreted as representing the duality of human beings. When Hutter first meets the vampire, isn't there a sort of symmetry (each framed by an arch) between them? When Ellen wakes up at night and reaches out across the screen, isn't it Nosferatu that turns towards her? Does she secretly desire him?

darkly erotic

When she sits by the sea and says to Ruth that she 'must go to him', whom does she mean? When she embroiders 'I love you', is it Hutter she refers to or her 'dark lover' who stares forlornly across to her and who will not come until she calls?

That Ellen dies at the end should, according to Phil Hardy (*Aurum Encyclopaedia of Horror*), make us question society's sexual double standards – she saves the town, but has become 'unclean' by taking the vampire into her bed; a fallen woman, she cannot be allowed to live.

In a recent newspaper article about *Nosferatu*, Christopher Frayling comments that Nosferatu resembles a 'nasty looking penis' (Frayling, 2001). When the vampire rises up abruptly from his coffin in the Empusa, doesn't it bear a striking similarity to an erection? He occupies vagina-like burrows and cleaves through the ocean. The rhythm of the waves evokes sexual intercourse. When Ellen reads the Book of Vampires she looks at it furtively as though it were pornography. Much of the action in the film occurs in bedrooms, and in the final scene Ellen clutches her breast, and shudders with what could be pain but might be pleasure, when his shadow travels up her body. Orgasm, in a French phrase, is a 'little death'. The Surrealists felt that the film was darkly erotic. American 'Beat' writer Jack Kerouac described the final scene between Ellen and the vampire as 'a horribly perverted love scene' (Kerouac, 1972).

The problem with such interpretations is that they can easily spiral out of control. Psychoanalysis is extremely diverse, with radically different schools, and some film critics use it without any formal training, plundering whatever concepts seem serviceable. What evidence can determine the truth of a particular interpretation?

Purely psychological accounts ignore historical and social factors. Writers who treat horror as trans-historical, as addressing timeless human fears, neglect the way in which horror films have changed in response to fears and anxieties specific to particular periods in time. Why did films like *Nosferatu* go out of fashion in Germany after 1924, precisely when the economy stabilised? Kim Newman (Newman, 1993) suggests that the horror film has always boomed at times of social crisis, but that each new wave has had features relevant to specific issues of that moment (for example, fears of Communism in the 1950s).

homosexual readings

Can *Nosferatu* be 'read' from a gay perspective? Some film theorists have brought a fresh approach to studies of films, film history and genres like horror by investigating their representations of 'deviant' sexuality.

For much of film history, homosexuality was only ever represented on screen in highly coded or stereotyped ways, and usually in a hostile tone. However, there were gay and lesbian directors who infused their films with a 'queer' sensibility while 'queer' audiences learnt to read 'between the lines' and 'against the grain' of even very conventional films in order to derive pleasure from them.

In the case of the horror genre, we know that some of the early directors and stars were gay (James Whale, the director of Universal's *Frankenstein*, for example), and the films often had a 'camp' atmosphere that gay audiences recognised and enjoyed. Years later, *The Rocky Horror Picture Show* spelled out the possible sub-text in the story of a male scientist engaged in creating his own, artificial man.

Harry Benshoff, in *Monsters in the closet*, suggests that horror films are particularly susceptible to 'queer readings' because they are inherently perverse. At the centre of horror films is a monster rejected by society, something with which homosexuals can identify.

German films of the 1920s contained many examples of cross-dressing, sexual masquerade and androgyny, as well as overt gay and lesbian themes (Richard Oswald's *Anders Als Die Andere* was one of the few films about homosexuality made in the silent era, while *Maidens in Uniform* narrates the dramatic consequences of a girl's 'crush' on a female teacher). Murnau was gay and American film-maker Stan Brakhage argues that the film has distinctly 'camp' elements (quoted in Bouvier and Leutrat, 1981). One can see Knock as procuring a young man for the pleasure of an older one. Several shots of Hutter (for example when he is asleep at Ellen's bedside in a soft light) present him in a homo-erotic way. Janet Bergstrom

Germany's rich tradition of fantasy

(Bergstrom, 1986), suggests that Murnau's films blur gender identities, with female characters often de-sexualised and men 'feminised'. When the supernatural coach races up the hill to Nosferatu's castle, and the coachman gestures imperiously, it has a melodramatic excess reminiscent of Gloria Swanson in *Sunset Boulevard*.

One of the remarkable features of *Nosferatu* is the way one comes to feel pity for him at the end. He seems so 'needy' and alone as he looks towards Ellen from his ruined warehouse home. He is the ultimate outsider. Did Murnau identify with the vampire's alienation as a gay man in a homophobic society?

nosferatu & cinema

Another interpretation is to see the film not as an expression of meanings derived from social history or human psychology, but in terms of cinema itself.

To begin with, one can see the film purely in terms of product differentiation in a competitive market. It's undeniable that one of the motives behind films like *Caligari* or *Nosferatu* was to attract an educated, middle class audience. One way to do this was to make films of an artistic kind. To distinguish German films in the international market place, what better than to draw on Germany's rich tradition of fantasy but also, in the case of *Nosferatu*, on a best-selling novel successful all over Europe? Erich Pommer, in interviews with George Huaco, stressed the economics of 'stylised films' (Huaco, 1965). Thomas Elsaesser has argued (Elsaesser, 2000) that one should not ignore the hard-headed decisions involved in film production, and how German film-makers of the 1920s had to negotiate the marketplace they confronted.

Another way to see *Nosferatu* in terms of cinema is to recognise it as reflexively 'about' the medium itself. The film delights in using cinematic trickery and the vampire is a very filmic creature, a thing of shadows. When he enters Hutter's bedroom it seems as though he is being borne on a beam of light from a projector; we see his shadow thrown onto the 'screen' of the bedhead and, later, onto the stairs to Ellen's room. One of Albin Grau's remarkable production sketches for the film features Ellen staring disbelievingly at the vampire as he transfixes her with beams of light from his eyes (included in Skal, 1990). At the end of the film he goes up like a puff of smoke as sunlight returns, just as a film disappears when the lights of the cinema are turned back on, and just as the nitrate film of the silent era can explode and be reduced to powder.

Murnau devoted his life to film-making; the Austrian writer Arnold Hollriegel wrote about him:

> he sees the world through the lens of a camera ... Murnau has become a new kind of being who thinks directly in photographs ... a kind of modern centaur; he and the camera are joined together to form a single body.
>
> *Hollywood Bilderbuch 1927, quoted in Eisner, 1973*

Rather than expressing himself, was Murnau simply taking pleasure in the artifice of film, in what he could do with it? Was the real subject of his work film itself?

A third possibility is that the film had satirical intentions. Conservative critics portrayed the cinema as a dangerous force, employing vampire metaphors to express their fears of its effects, particularly on female spectators; was Murnau mischievously provoking them by enacting their worst nightmares on the screen?

conclusion

In *Weimar Cinema and after*, Elsaesser comments that the directors who made the great German films of the 1920s were more intelligent, witty and ironic than the people who have written about them. Murnau, Lang and Lubitsch lived in a time of intense contradictions, rapid social change and violent polarities; perhaps they had to be elusive to survive. To encourage, but also to frustrate, the search for meaning in a film, leaves an audience dizzy; identities are provisional and conclusions unstable. Was this what they really wanted to say?

bibliography

general film

Altman, Rick, *Film Genre*, BFI, 1999
Detailed exploration of the concept of film genre

Bordwell, David, *Narration in the Fiction Film*, Routledge, 1985
A detailed study of narrative theory and structures

– – –, Staiger, Janet & Thompson, Kristin, *The Classical Hollywood Cinema: Film Style & Mode of Production to 1960*, Routledge, 1985; pbk 1995
An authoritative study of cinema as institution, it covers film style and production

– – – & Thompson, Kristin, *Film Art*, McGraw-Hill, 4th edn, 1993
An introduction to film aesthetics for the non-specialist

Branson, Gill & Stafford, Roy, *The Media Student's Handbook*, Routledge, 2nd edn, 1999

Buckland, Warren, *Teach Yourself Film Studies*, Hodder & Stoughton, 1998
Very accessible, it gives an overview of key areas in film studies

Cook, Pam & Bernink, Mieke (eds), *The Cinema Book*, BFI, 2nd edn, 1999

Corrigan, Tim, *A Short Guide To Writing About Film*, HarperCollins, 1994
What it says: a practical guide for students

Dyer, Richard (with Paul McDonald), *Stars*, BFI, 2nd edn, 1998
A good introduction to the star system

Easthope, Antony, *Classical Film Theory*, Longman, 1993
A clear overview of writing about film theory

Hayward, Susan, *Key Concepts in Cinema Studies*, Routledge, 1996

Hill, John & Gibson, Pamela Church (eds), *The Oxford Guide to Film Studies*, Oxford University Press, 1998
Wide-ranging standard guide

Kennedy, Harlan, 'Kiltspotting: Highland Reels', in *Film Comment* vol.32 no.4, July-August 1996
An analysis of the style and themes of 1990s' Scottish films

Lapsley, Robert & Westlake, Michael, *Film Theory: An Introduction*, Manchester University Press, 1994

Maltby, Richard & Craven, Ian, *Hollywood Cinema*, Blackwell, 1995
A comprehensive work on the Hollywood industry and its products

McArthur, Colin, 'The Cultural Necessity of a Poor Celtic Cinema', in *Border Crossings: Film in Ireland, Britain and Europe*, John Hill, Martin McLoone and Paul Hainsworth (eds), BFI, 1994
A polemical argument about how Scottish cinema should be organised in order not to lose sight of specifically Scottish concerns

Mulvey, Laura, 'Visual Pleasure and Narrative Cinema' (1974), in *Visual and Other Pleasures*, Indiana University Press, Bloomington, 1989
The classic analysis of 'the look' and 'the male gaze' in Hollywood cinema. Also available in numerous other edited collections

Nelmes, Jill (ed.), *Introduction to Film Studies*, Routledge, 2nd edn, 1999
Deals with several national cinemas and key concepts in film study

Nowell-Smith, Geoffrey (ed.),
The Oxford History of World Cinema,
Oxford University Press, 1996
Hugely detailed and wide-ranging
with many features on 'stars'

**Roddick, Nick, 'Show Me the
Culture!',** in *Sight and Sound* vol.8
no.12, December 1998
A polemical argument about the state
of the British film industry in the late
1990s and the type of film making
this encourages

**Thomson, David, *A Biographical
Dictionary of the Cinema,***
Secker & Warburg, 1975
Unashamedly driven by personal taste,
but often stimulating

Truffaut, François, *Hitchcock,*
Simon & Schuster, 1966,
rev. edn. Touchstone, 1985
Landmark extended interview

Turner, Graeme, *Film as Social Practice,*
3rd edn, Routledge, 1999
Chapter four, 'Film Narrative',
discusses structuralist theories of
narrative

**Wollen, Peter, *Signs and Meaning in
the Cinema,*** BFI 1997 (revised edn)
An important study in semiology

Readers should also explore the many
relevant websites and journals.

Film Education and *Sight and Sound*
are standard reading.

Valuable websites include:

The Internet Movie Database at
www.uk.imdb.com

Screensite at
www.tcf.ua.edu/screensite/contents.html

The Media and Communications Site
at the University of Aberystwyth at
www.aber.ac.uk/~dgc/welcome.html

There are obviously many other
university and studio websites which
are worth exploring in relation to film
studies.

nazism

Brustein, W., *The Logic of Evil,*
Yale University Press, 1996
Analyses the appeal of Nazism to the
material self-interest of different
sections of the German population

the horror film

**Benshoff, H., *Monsters in the
Closet,*** Manchester University Press,
1997
Interprets horror films from a gay
perspective

Carroll, N., *The Philosophy of Horror,*
Routledge, 1990
A fascinating study of the cognitive
pleasures of horror and its
characteristic plots

nosferatu & german cinema of the 1920s

Arnold, L., Farin, M. and Schmid, H., *Nosferatu*, Belleville, Munich, 2000

Barlow, John, *German Expressionist Film*, Twayne, Boston, 1982

Bergstom, J., 'Sexuality at a Loss: the films of Murnau', in *The Female Body in Western Culture*, Suleiman, S. (ed.), Harvard University Press, 1986

Berriatua, L., *Los Proverbios Chinos de F.W. Murnau – etapa alemana*, Filmoteca Espanola, 1990

Bouvier, M. and Leutrat, J.-L., *Nosferatu*, Cahiers du Cinema / Seuil, 1981
> Two leading French critics analyse the film. It contains a wealth of information and a valuable selection of reviews, essays about the film, and articles by key players like Albin Grau

Collier, Jo Ann, *From Wagner to Murnau*, UMI Research Press, Ann Arbor, 1988
> Places Murnau in a tradition of German Romantic theatre and music

Dalle Vache, A., *Cinema and Painting*, University of Texas Press, 1996

Eisner, Lotte, *The Haunted Screen*, Thames & Hudson, London, 1969
> Essential reading on the German cinema of the Weimar period. Beautifully illustrated with stills

Eisner, Lottle, *Murnau*, Secker and Warburg, London, 1973
> Out of print; a major biography of the director. Contains the shooting script of *Nosferatu*

Elsaesser, Thomas, *Weimar Cinema and After*, Routledge, 2000
> The most important book on Weimar cinema in recent years. Aims to open up the period to post-Kracauer interpretations. Excellent chapter on Murnau

Elsaesser, Thomas, 'Six degrees of Murnau', in *Sight and Sound*, Feb 2000

Gelder, K., *Reading the Vampire*, Routledge, 1994

Hardy, P., *The Aurum Film Encyclopaedia: Horror*, Aurum 1985

Huaco, G., *The Sociology of Film Art*, Basic Books, New York, 1965

Kael, P., *5001 Nights at the Movies*, Marion Boyars, 1993

Kerouac, J., 'Nosferatu', in *Authors on Film*, Geduld, Y. (ed.), Indiana University, 1972

Koszarski, R., *Hollywood Directors 1914–40*, Oxford University Press, 1976

Kracauer, S., *From Caligari to Hitler*, Princeton University Press, 1947
> For years this was considered the definitive account of the social meaning of Weimar cinema. Recent scholars are critical of his methodology

Kracauer, S., *The Mass Ornament*, Harvard, 1995

Kurtz, R., *Expressionismus und Film*, Lichtbildbuhne, Berlin, 1926

Petro, P., *Joyless Streets*, Princeton University Press, 1989

Roth, L., 'Dracula meets the Zeitgeist: Nosferatu (1922) as Film Adaptation', in *Literature/Film Quarterly*, 7, No. 4, 1979

Roud, R., *Cinema: A Critical Dictionary*, Secker & Warburg, 1980

Salt, B., 'From Caligari to Who?', in *Sight & Sound*, Spring 1979

Salt, Barry, *Film Style and Technology: History & Analysis*, Starword, 1983

Shepard, J., *Nosferatu in Love*, Faber & Faber, 1998
    A highly readable novelisation of Murnau's life

Skal, D., *Hollywood Gothic*, Deutsch, London, 1990
    Although principally about Hollywood's first Dracula film, contains a lively account of *Nosferatu* and includes some of Grau's amazing production sketches

Sklar, R., *Film: An International History of the Medium*, Thames & Hudson, 1993

Stümke, H., 'The Persecution of Homosexuals in Nazi Germany', in *Confronting the Nazi Past*, Burleigh, M. (ed.), Collins and Brown, 1996

Wollenberg, H., *Fifty Years of German Cinema*, Falcon Press, 1948
    Out of print; concise account of early German cinema from an economic perspective

Wood, R., *Murnau, Midnight and Sunrise*, Film Comment 3, 1976

Wood, R., *The American Nightmare*, Festival of Festivals, Toronto, 1979

cinematic terms

180 degree rule when shooting a scene between two people, one must stay to one side of an invisible line between them when moving the camera; if not, they will appear on screen to have exchanged places, confusing the audience

accelerated motion when screen action seems speeded-up; achieved in the silent era by under-cranking the camera

auteur a film-maker with artistic integrity, whose work expresses the director's vision of life and recognisable visual style

camera angle the camera can look at a subject from above, from below, at eye level etc.

chiaroscuro a play of light and shade

cinematographer professional responsible for camera, lighting, film stock etc.

close-up a shot that focuses on a specific object. In the case of a person, a close-up frames the head and neck, a **medium close-up** includes the chest, and an **extreme close-up** is very close to the subject (e.g. the eyes)

closure a narrative has closure when it ends in a way that seems to tie up all the loose ends satisfactorily

continuity editing when shots are edited together to make action flow logically and naturally

cut a simple, abrupt transition from one shot to another

deep focus when everything in a scene, from near to far, is sharp

diegesis the world of the narrative (so that 'diegetic sound' is sound belonging to the action in the story; a 'diegetic narrator' is one of the characters)

establishing shot a shot which sets up a scene by showing the audience where subsequent action takes place

eyeline match when two shots of different characters are composed so that when edited together there appears to be eye contact

high angle shot a shot that looks down on a subject

inter-title in silent films, dialogue and other information appears on screen

intertextuality many media texts quote from, refer to, parody other media texts

iris in/iris out in silent cinema it was very common to begin and end scenes with shots in which an image grows from a small circle against a black background to fill the screen, and vice versa

jump cut an edit which is not seamless, but is discontinuous

long shot also called a wide shot, this shows a subject from a distance; in the case of a person, a long shot shows the whole body; an extreme long shot dwarfs a subject in its environment

low angle shot a shot that looks up at a subject

medium shot a shot that gives us a degree of intimacy with a subject, but is neither close nor distant – in the case of a person, from the waist up

mise-en-scène some writers use this to refer to sets, lighting, arrangement of performers only; others also include the camera movements relative to the performers and sets

cinematic terms

montage editing images not to convey a particular piece of continuous action, but to juxtapose images separated in space and time so as to summarise time periods or develop a theme

pan a camera movement that scans a scene (surveying pan) or follows a moving object (following pan)

parallel action this exists when more than one line of action is developed at the same time, and the film crosscuts between them

plot the sequence used to tell the story; this may be the same as the chronological story, but need not be. The plot may shift events to create suspense, shock etc.

reach when used about narrative, refers to the extent of information that the audience has

realism some films aspire to be true to life, plausible etc.

shallow focus selective focus; only objects at a certain distance from the camera are sharp

stop-motion the basis of animation; the camera is stopped, an adjustment made to an object, another shot taken etc. – projected normally, it fools the eye into seeing continuous motion

superimposition when more than one image is visible on screen at the same time

vertical integration when a company controls production, distribution and exhibition of films, it is vertically integrated

credits

title

Nosferatu – A Symphony of Horror

production company

Prana-Film

Released 4 March 1922 in Berlin, Germany

director

Friedrich Wilhelm Murnau

screenplay

Henrik Galeen

Based on the novel by Bram Stoker

photography

Fritz Arno Wagner

Gunther Krampf

editor

F.W. Murnau

music

Hans Erdmann

art design, costumes and sets

Albin Grau

length

1967 metres

cast

Count Orlok – Max Schreck

Hutter – Gustav von Wangenheim

Ellen, Hutter's wife – Greta Schroeder

Knock, an estate agent – Alexander Granach

Harding, a shipbuilder – G.H. Schnell

Ruth, Harding's sister – Ruth Landshoff

Professor Sievers, municipal doctor – Gustav Botz

Professor Bulwer, a Paracelsian – John Gottowt

Captain – Max Nemetz

1st Sailor – Wolfgang Heinz

2nd Sailor – Albert Venohr